MARGUERITE

JOURNEY OF A
SEPHARDIC WOMAN

A Memoir by

Gloria Sananes Stein

MARGUERITE
Journey of a Sephardic Woman

Printed in the United States of America.

Library of Congress Number: 97-73544

International Standard Book Number: 1-883294-52-5

Published by
Masthof Press
Route 1, Box 20, Mill Road
Morgantown, PA 19543

DEDICATION

MARGUERITE

IS DEDICATED

TO MY CHILDREN,

JON, BOB AND CAROL

AND TO ARNOLD,

MY HUSBAND,

MY EDITOR

AND MY BEST FRIEND.

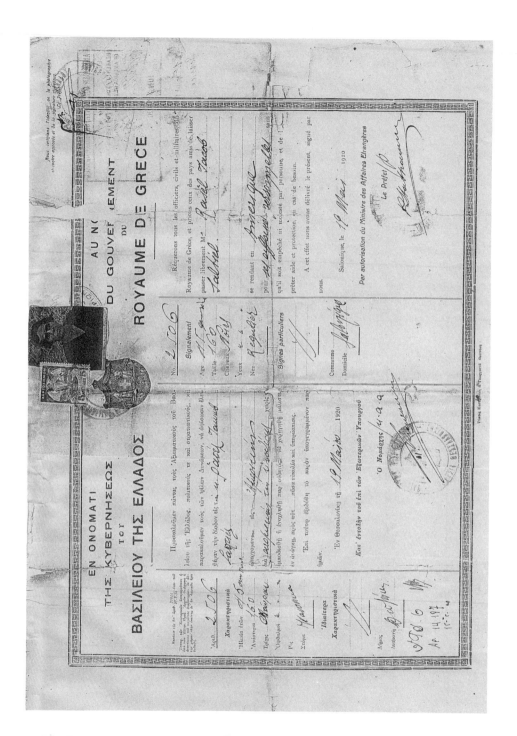

Passport

CONTENTS

ACKNOWLEDGEMENTS

I wish to thank Bob Bedford and the Foundation for the Advancement of Sephardic Studies for their support throughout the development of this book.

I am grateful to The Friends of L'Alliance Universelle for their support and maps of the Mediterranean.

Without my sisters Clarice Nahum, Ethel Kubie and Charlotte Russell, the book would not have been possible. Many of their recollections were unknown to me.

Clarie provided historical materials from her personal library and was tireless in gathering information and photographs and recording her experience with Mom.

My "big sister" Essie, the eldest, has been Mom's constant companion. Essie heard the tales of the other side many more times than anyone else. She was the one who has shared Mom's youth as well as her old age.

Charlotte sat down one dreary day and wrote her reminiscences which further fleshed out the woman we all love.

I wish to thank my nephew James Russell and niece Michelle Albright for their fond memories of Grandma's love and wisdom, and for appreciating the good food from her kitchen.

Along with the history of the family I have included recipes, a few songs and many Ladino expressions, as Mom expressed them; without them there would only be a skeleton memoir. Some names have been changed to protect their identity.

Most of all I want to thank my husband, Arnold Stein, who tirelessly reviewed my research, read each chapter and pointed me in the right direction.

Prologue

Mas vale una dracma de mazal que una oca de ducados.

**A single ounce of luck is worth more
than a whole pile of money.**

Back in the 1940s, Mom loved to watch her four daughters gather in the kitchen, sing, tell jokes, tease and dreamily plan a future of love, marriage and career. Fifty years later we have gathered once again in Mama's kitchen to recapture some of the past and recall her spirit and dignity.

For over five years we sat at her bedside, watching her frail body become crippled with arthritis as inarticulate wails and cries faded into multiple strokes. But the body, even in its dark space, kept its own time as she endured the aches, breaks and pinches which suddenly seized her and then subsided.

Marguerite Saltiel Sananes was a woman who spoke English, Greek, French and Italian. Withered hands, which became more like claws, were once warm and comforting, spreading a blanket of security. Hers was the voice that sang lullabies and French songs of promised love. She admonished in Ladino, told stories and freely gave advice in several languages.

As she washed dishes she would often lapse into stories of her years as a writer. "Gloria, please tell my story, *Yo tuve mazal*, I had luck."

Proud to be part of the wave of immigration, Marguerite believed that she had made it in America. By some standards she didn't. Neither rich or powerful, she didn't achieve any scandal-worthy notoriety and, although schooled in suffering, did not face overwhelming tragedy. She never saw America's great plains, western canyons, buttes or towering redwoods, but she made this her land the day she set foot on its sidewalks; she was the most patriotic of women, a heroine of her own life story.

But getting here, staying here, owning a home, marrying an American businessman, raising four daughters, watching them get a good education and prosper was, to her, immeasurable success. Although Mom didn't have a longing to belong, she boasted to the world about her daughters. "My girls are the best," she often said. "Everyone on the block is jealous of me because of my girls. *Son mi riqueza,* they are my riches."

On visits to Mom's home in Brooklyn, we explored the depths of our memories as we recalled her story and ours, reminiscences of poverty and despair, survival and success and the progress of many lives.

Like a squirrel with a food stash, she had a proverb in either Ladino (Judeo-Espanyol) or French for every occasion.

Be honest: *La mentira tiene pies curtos* (falsehood has short legs).

Choose friends carefully: *Dime con quien conoscas, te dire quien sois* (tell me who you know and I'll tell you who you are).

The stories generated strength. We listened to folklore, the tales of *johar*, the fool, and the wise people who straightened out the world and gave it meaning.

Collecting Life Stories

As people collect antiques to touch the past, Marguerite's daughters have gathered to collect the life affirming acts she instilled in our behavior. Sheltered by her arms as children, we were later sheltered in her thoughts, following her figurative compass. Who we are is part of who she was as she remains our spiritual salt.

I look at her passport photo, the earliest we have. At 18, I can see her boarding the ship for America docked at Piraeus, the port of embarkation near Athens. Her head is wrapped in a black scarf. A gold medallion, a prize for scholarship, hangs from her neck, giving some brilliance to the simple black dress.

Barely out of her teens she has become a woman, leading a family on a crossing to safety, to reclaim their lives in a new land, taking more risks, after the experience of war, fire and survival.

Knowing Marguerite is to understand her against the canvas of her time: a young woman struggling with shifting social, political and economic conditions. In the process of writing this memoir, speaking with family members, probing the past, recalling the uniqueness of our language and rediscovering Mom's cooking, I have come to know my mother and my sisters through a personal prism in a thousand ways that eluded me when I was younger.

As the words I gathered transformed into chapters, I was convinced that if I didn't write down who we were, our children and our children's children would never grasp the essence of this strand of their past. Readers curious about a piece of the American mosaic can now enter the world of a culture that is often relegated to a footnote of world history.

Mom died at the age of 96. Her funeral, which was held on a freezing day in January, 1996, brought together the people who knew her well. As we ritually picked up handfuls of soil to toss on her grave, we sensed that she had found peace at last. One week after her death my fourth granddaughter, Mara was born, named according to Jewish tradition in respect for her great-grandmother Marguerite.

NOTES

Some of the idioms in this book are virtually impossible to translate, but I try to capture the tempo and spirit of the sayings. Knowing a little Spanish might make some of these easily pronounceable bon mots more significant, but it isn't necessary.

Sephardim: Term refers to the descendants of the Jews who lived in Spain and Portugal during the Middle Ages, until persecution cul-minating in expulsion forced them to leave.

Ashkenazim: Members of a branch of European Jews, historically Yiddish speaking, who settled in central and northern Europe.

A few names have been changed to protect individuals' privacy.

Appreciation is given to Robert Bedford of The Foundation for the Advancement of Sephardic Studies and Culture, Brooklyn, NY, for the photographs on pages 8, 13, 24, and 48.

SPAIN

Sephardim comes from the Hebrew word for Spain.

Marguerite Saltiel was born in Salonica in 1900 when the city was under the rule of the Ottoman Empire. For 400 years the huge Jewish quarter was largely populated by descendants of the Spanish inquisition that drove Jews to all corners of the Mediterranean in the 15th century.

Her mother, Rachel Benrube, born in 1868, and her father, Jacob Saltiel, born in 1865, lived in the nation that was ruled by the Turks. Salonica at the beginning of the 20th century was a "Jewish" city with 80,000 Sephardim out of 150,000 residents.

The Sephardim played such an important role in commerce and culture that work came to a halt on Saturdays and holy days. "The Turks were good to us," recalled Grandma. "We had no trouble with them or the Greeks when the city was turned over in 1912." In spite of the Balkan Wars and the First World War, the large Jewish population was content to live in peace in the land which had offered them refuge.

EXPULSION

On March 31, 1492, as Christopher Columbus was kneeling before the throne of King Ferdinand and Queen

1

Decree of Granada

Isabella, the royal couple were signing the Decree of Granada, expelling the Jews from Spain. They sought to justify the action by arguing that Jews continued to proselytize among former Jews who had converted to Christianity (*los conversos*).

Since the 10th century, Jews as men of letters were influential with diplomats, jurists, translators and financial experts, often linked to Spanish courts and Arab rulers. It was indeed a rare period when Jews, Christians and Muslims lived in harmony under Moorish rule. In Moslem Spain the Jews rose up and volunteered aid to the Moslems in their war of conquest. This emphasizes a special character in the Jewish community which had no parallel in the history of other diaspora communities. Later on, the Christians gradually reclaimed Spain.

By the 14th century, resentment against Jews became apparent and pogroms were in force by 1391. In 1480 in Toledo, all Jews in cities, towns and kingdoms were ordered to separate, assigned special areas to reside. An inquisition was carried out by secular and religious people for 12 years which found many people guilty of subverting the holy Catholic faith, attracting others to the "accursed beliefs" of Moslems and Jews. Thousands perished.

Whereas in other lands Jews only defended themselves when attacked, the Jews of Spain were accustomed to participate in wars and to defend the lands they inhabited. Spanish Jews did not look upon themselves as foreign colonists but as an indigenous element of the country whose livelihood depended on agriculture and who adopted the lifestyle of local citizens. There are striking parallels between the Jews of Spain and the Israeli struggle to protect their lands.

After the fall of Granada and the ouster of Muslims, the legendary Torquemada and the Inquisitor General demanded total expulsion.

By the 15th century the Roman Catholic Church under increased pressure from Christian reformers used Jews and Muslims as convenient scapegoats and pushed towards conversion. While thousands reluctantly converted in Spain's effort to unify the nation religiously, over 300,000 fled.

All Jewish men, women, sons, daughters, relatives and servants were compelled to leave and never return under penalty of death. To expedite expulsion, the royals even allowed exiles a chance to sell what they owned. Of the estimated 200-300,000 souls who fled, 25,000 Jews from Spain and Portugal settled in Salonica.

Family history indicates that my grandmother's line is from Seville, my grandfather's from Toledo and my father's from Salamanca. The Saltiels and the Sananes' always thought of themselves as Spanish-Jews first and citizens of their adopted country second. After 400 years of expulsion, they maintained strong emotional connections to Spain.

While the Spanish Inquisition is most noted in Jewish history, it was not the first. England expelled Jews in 1290, France in 1394 and Portugal followed Spain in 1496. The flight from Spain was more disruptive because communities were larger and more settled than anywhere else in Europe.

Initially the exiles found their way to Constantinople, where they were welcomed by Turkish rulers, but later settled in Balkan Lands and North Africa. Their new life was made easier with the support of the Ottoman Empire which extended from what is now Turkey to the Crimea, Moldova, Romania, Bulgaria, Serbia, Bosnia, Greece and Albania. It was the Sephardim who brought the first printing press to the Ottoman Empire and within two years of settlement published the first Hebrew book in 1494.

Membership in one of the many synagogues in Salonica was often based on the area of Spain from which Jews had fled. Among the treasures of these temples were objects hidden during expulsion. The 1917 fire in Salonica destroyed many of these prized possessions which attested to the glory of the Jewish presence in Spain.

To the Ashkenazim of Northern Europe who shared the same religion, the Sephardim with their particular rituals seemed different, at times exotic. Their food and music was more Mediterranean and Ladino; the language they carried with them into exile appeared unintelligible.

Conversations with Sephardi in our home always revealed an unusual resilience. How could Spanish Jews who had felt the sting of antisemitism and were expelled from lands where they left an imprint of knowledge and commitment continue to hold their heads up high?

According to Sephardic psychiatrist Dr. Martin B. Sevilya, these Jews were steadfast in their faith and full of determination to preserve their identity. Each crisis was like a purifying experience; the more they were struck, the stronger and more united they became.

Dr. Sevilya noted that the Sephardim had a capacity for healthy adaptation to many different and difficult conditions. They did this by neutralizing the aggressive

4

forces with *hohma* (wisdom). By so doing they were able to preserve a vital equilibrium, compromising psychologically with inner and outer conflicts, as they adjusted to everyday life in their struggle for survival.

The Jews who left Spain at various times can be classified as medieval and Renaissance Jews. Those who remained behind after the expulsion of 1492 as Neo-Christians (Conversos) came under the power of religion and culture denied to those who had fled. It was in this time of enlightenment that Spain was influenced by world-wide cultural currents.

When these cultured Conversos, also known as Peninsular Jews, eventually reclaimed their Jewish heritage and settled in Italian cities, southern France, England, Holland, Germany and the far flung regions of the new world such as Jamaica, Curacao and New Amsterdam in America, they brought with them the traditions of Catholic Spain and Portugal.

Of the many Jewish languages and dialects, Judeo-Espanyol (Ladino) prevailed. Studies reveal that the sheer numbers of Spanish exiles impacted on the Jewish communities already in existence in Ottoman held lands.

These exiles, bearers of rabbinic, Hebraic and European intellectual traditions, were culturally more advanced than indigenous Ottoman Jews or the Turkish conquerors. Thus they clung to their language rather than assimilate. In countries occupied by people with many diverse languages, and where social segregation was encouraged, it was easy for the Spanish-Jews to hold on to their heritage. The predominance of Ladino in their community allowed them to maintain contacts in business and trade with Sephardim in neighboring nations.

Unfortunately, the culture of medieval Jews was virtually ignored by historians as merely an incident in history. Remnants of a once glorious people, they did not fit into the larger concerns of Russian, German and American Jewry or the issues of Zionism.

Yet, it was this tradition of compromise and adaptation which helped my mother and her family come to terms with their circumstances. They were able to draw strength from their identity in Salonica to forge a successful life in America, only looking back with nostalgia, not regret.

SALONICA

Jewish Presence in Greece

Our family was rarely bored. Winter afternoons in the 1940s were spent sitting with my grandmother as she crocheted a lace collar or sewed a hem. Her hands were always busy, and our smaller hands reached out to join in the activity.

Mom washed old wool from worn sweaters and spent hours making new recycled balls. The children knitted, crocheted and embroidered as we listened to another chapter in the life of our family in Salonica. It was never planned or rehearsed, just a description of *Como era al tiempo de mi padre*, what daily life was like in the time of our forefathers in the latter part of the 19th century.

Many a tale began with, *al tiempo de los Turkos* (in the era of the Turks) or *antes de los Turkos* (before the Turks).

As early as the 3rd century BC, the faithful worshipped at the temple of Zeus and the Jews were in alliance with Sparta, the traditional foe of Athens. Even earlier there were Jewish settlements on the islands of Delos and Kos and cities like Athens and Salonica.

Philo who lived two generations before the destruction of the Second Temple, mentioned that Jewish communities worshipped in synagogues in the kingdoms of Macedonia,

Salonica woman.
Courtesy of Robert Bedford, The
Foundation for the Advancement
of Sephardic Studies and Culture.

Jewish merchant in Salonica.
Courtesy of Robert Bedford, The Foun-
dation for the Advancement of
Sephardic Studies and Culture.

8

Thessaly and Corinth. Although Jewish life flourished in areas under the Greeks and Romans, it received a severe setback when Byzantium embraced Christianity. As in Spain, thousands were then forcibly converted to the new religion.

A Romaniote Jewish community centered around Ionnina as early as 3rd century BC still exists, although 2000 people were deported to Auschwitz during the Holocaust. The population has now dwindled to 100 souls, yet there are many in Israel that support a Romaniot synagogue.

The tides of fortune changed once again for Jews when the Turks captured Constantinople in 1453 and established the Ottoman Empire in the Balkans, including Greece.

What did families fleeing Spain find when they arrived in 1492? In addition to Romaniotes (Greek-speaking), they found Ashkenazi-Germanic (Yiddish speaking) Jews and even a group of Catalan-speaking Jews from the Balearic Islands. It did not take long for the word to get around of the attractiveness and calm that prevailed in Salonica. The exiles, former teachers, bankers, state officials, physicians, scholars and craftsmen brought an infusion of new life to Salonica, a former sumptuous Byzantine metropolis that had declined to a sleepy port.

Although the Turks ruled by theocracy (Islam), it was with a spirit of tolerance that Mohammed II, conqueror of Constantinople, in 1453 approached the governing of new subjects. Granting each religious group virtual autonomy, he made leaders responsible for the government and conduct of their people. Jews, Greeks and Turks lived within their own spheres, although subgroups like the Serbs, Bulgarians and

Vlachs who were ethnically distinct were grouped under the power of Greek bishops.

Under Islamic rule, Turkish commitment to receive the exiles with kindness and assistance allowed Jews to flourish once again until the Greek Wars of Liberation. These wars, which began in 1821 finally led to the overthrow of an already waning Ottoman power. Yet, while liberation was justifiably precious to Christian Greeks, it brought mistreatment and misunderstanding for those Greeks who were Jews.

Jews faced incidents of antisemitism throughout their period of exile. In the 1820s, when the Turkish Janisaries (elite guards) were putting down the revolt of the Greeks, they killed the Patriarch Gregory in cold blood and then forced several Jews to throw the body into the sea. When news of this outrage reached the Greeks of Morea, it wasn't the Turks but the Jews who were blamed and massacred to the last man.

In the 19th century, the port city of Salonica was one of the most important commercial centers of European trade. The Jews who comprised over half the population were steadily becoming westernized, having already gained some control of the economic life of the booming metropolis. Visits from foreign travelers, foreign language schools and stories from abroad drove the people to expand their horizons.

With a few words in one language and the addition of a few in another, the language underwent enormous changes with 400 years of Turkish influence in addition to French and Greek vocabulary among other idioms. Judeo-Espanyol as spoken in the early 19th century differed somewhat from the idiom at the close of the century but was distinctly Castillian.

The multiethnic nature of the empire, the existence of many different educational systems associated with different religious and ethnic minorities, the relative weakness of the Ottoman infrastructure, all contributed to the relative slowness of assimilation among the Sephardim. The strong sense of a distinct Sephardi identity remained intact.

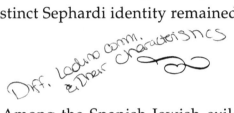

Diff. Ladino comm. & Their Characteristics

Among the Spanish-Jewish exiles the descendants of Aragones from the interior of Spain were thought of as traditionalists. Domineering, proud and stubborn, they were labeled cold, self centered, lazy and apathetic.

According to folklore, there were many internal prejudices among the various groups of Spanish exiles. The Catalans, a seacoast people, were characterized as alert, friendly, polished, hard working and intelligent. Grandpa used to say, "*Los Catalanes, de las piedras sacan panes*" (the Catalans can extract bread from stones). Those who emigrated from Galicia and lived in the *cortijos* (quarters) of the poor were defined as simple folk, long suffering and sober. Their rural dialect, difficult to understand was captured in the saying, *somos Gallegos, no nos entendemos* (we are Gallegos and are not understood).

However, it was the Castillians, the largest group and the culture of my mother and her family that set the tone for everything, including language, customs and manners.

The various groups self-segregated by province of origin elected their own presidents and erected their own synagogues. Eventually they merged into one large community under the leadership of Raphael Asher Covo and established a fiscal system and judicial courts as well as commercial consulates in the principal Italian ports.

"Fue Don Senor Benviste, ijo de los ricos que empezo todo (it was the rich Beneviste who began everything)," said Grandma. Don Senor Benviste, son of a former finance minister of Spain, founded schools, libraries and academies as well as a theological seminary and a medical school. As early as 1515 printing presses published theological, scientific and philosophical treatises.

Names were important in the Jewish fraternity then as now. Lines of history indicate that Freddy Abravanel who has worked with the Jewish Museum in Greece and is a native of Salonica is a direct descendant of Don Isaac Abravanel, a financial adviser to Ferdinand and Isabella. Among the Saloniklis, it was said, *basta el nombre de Abravanel* (just the name Abravanel is enough) to assure one's eminence in the community.

Jewish capital and expertise was tapped in the exportation of grain, wine, beer, textiles and tobacco. French instead of Spanish, which was the lingua franca, became the language of instruction. Many upper class families abandoned the local language at home in favor of French, *pero la mayoria ablaban Judeo-Espanyol*, but the masses reverted to dialect in daily conversation.

When asked, "Who are you?" the Jews of the city would answer, "I am neither a Turkish-Jew nor a Greek-Jew, but a native of Salonica."

It was in Salonica that journalistic and literary activity flourished in Judeo Espanyol and later in French. The press

12

Small children selling the Jewish newspaper, L'Indépendent, *which printed articles that my mom wrote.* Courtesy of Robert Bedford, The Foundation for the Advancement of Sephardic Studies and Culture.

which was crucial in establishing Sephardi culture also enlightened its readers to the European literary genre. When Mom wanted to make a point, she would say, *"el frances dice"* (as the French say) and that settled the problem. To her, their culture was full of wisdom and represented the final word on anything!

French classics were translated into Judeo Espanyol, and by the first decade of the 20th century, *Le Journal Salonique* catered to the Jewish population. Saadi Levy, a self-taught printer and agent of progress in Salonica, founded the great Judeo Espanyol newspaper *La Epoca*.

It was Mom's fascination with reading, writing and French literature that led to her employment with the small but popular newspaper, *L'Indépendent*. This major step eventually facilitated the family's emigration to America and ultimately to the salvation of an entire generation.

13

ANCESTORS

My grandfather, Jacob Saltiel, was born in 1865. We know that his father was Avram, a grain merchant, and his mother's name was Gracia. Jacob had two brothers, Ovadiah and Samuel. Avram, unlovingly called *Avram el malo*, was a classy but nasty, mean man.

Gracia was married at the young age of 13 to another teenager. On a trip to Palestine, the young man died from sun stroke before the couple had any children. To remarry, the bride had to get permission or *halitza* if she was a childless widow.

When a neighbor who served as a matchmaker was asked for a suitable second husband for the young woman, the neighbor said, "*yo lo tengo, un ombre bueno.*" The good man turned out to be the hot tempered Avram, prone to epileptic seizures. The young bride who had outgrown the trousseau provided for her childhood marriage now had to deal with a difficult husband.

"Nothing was ever recorded for women, it was all guesswork," said Mama. "Boys, since they were to be bar mitzvahed, had a more accurate idea of when they were born." In figuring birth dates the family would try to pinpoint an historic event like a fire, a crisis or the visit of a dignitary.

The name Saltiel is ancient, dating to the Golden Age in Spain. Legend has it, that in 1410, a Jewess named Maria *salto* (jumped) from a cloister wall in Segovia to escape conversion. The woman became known as *Maria del Salto*. Throughout history the Saltiel family were recognized as prominent businessmen and leaders particularly in Salonica, where they were members of Synagogue Mayor.

Papa (my grandfather), as was customary under Turkish rule, wore a *fez* and spoke many different languages. He was a merchant who bought and sold grain futures. A genius at math, he easily calculated everything in his head. Papa was a natural linguist who spoke French, Italian, Turkish, Bulgarian and Albanian in addition to Judeo Espanyol. In time he was able to communicate in English as he sought employment in New York City.

Rachel Benrube, my grandmother, was born in 1868. Her mother was Gracia Nachmas, and her father, Baruch.

Both of my grandparents were literate in Italian, since they attended the only schools available to them at the time.

Rachel, a career woman, wasn't married by her late 20s. The family worried that she would turn out to be *"una mosa vieja"* (old maid). Independent and feisty, she owned her own business, adamantly unwilling to be matched with a convenient husband who would prove unsuitable for the rest of her life.

The family knew that she wasn't strong, menstruated late and suffered from malnutrition and anemia. More importantly, she couldn't come up with an impressive dowry for the kind of man she would be willing to marry.

As a poor young girl, my grandmother was apprenticed to an Italian dressmaker who came to Salonica to clothe the elegant women of the embassies. Although it was a given that

15

every Jewish woman was also a seamstress, she extended her skills and soon learned enough to begin a small business of her own, helping to support the family with the help of apprentices.

"*El colliar es lo mas importante*," warned the Italian tailor, if the collar wasn't right, the dress was wrong. She never forgot the words of her mentor as she carefully fingered each collar, making sure the edges were knife-crisp before attaching to her dress.

As she took expensive, elegant samples of clothing apart and reproduced the designs, Grandma took on apprentices who helped mass produce clothing for the "cigarette girls," factory workers who lived in the city.

Poor but elegant, my grandmother maintained her dignity, strutting proudly through the Jewish quarter of the city, always beautifully attired, a walking advertisement of her skills.

Clothes, then as now, defined the status and class of its wearers. The Jewish women replicated the Ottoman dress which combined medieval, Islamic and Byzantine features. As subjects of the Sultan they were not allowed to dress in Frankish (European) style.

For Jews, the provincial nature of the city and the need to avoid attracting attention resulted in male clothing that was unpretentious for its time.

My grandfather socialized with men in the *kavanes* (cafes) where he rolled cigarettes with *tootoon* (tobacco), nibbled on *mezelik* (hors d'oeuvres) or traded on the market. In his long *yatari* or *camisa*, a long shirt worn over knee length pants (*pernil*) and an overgarment *bini* trimmed with fur, he was easily recognized for his status and class. Under Turkish rule, the mandated tall *fez* was worn by all men. Rabbis wore a *bonette*, a cap-like thick-brimmed headdress.

For many years we heard about the luxury of the "costumes" worn by Grandma and the women in her family.

"My *entari* was a close-fitting caftan with wide sleeves made of a striped silk material which covered undergarments consisting of *kalson* or bloomers," she said. "We didn't wear a brassiere like you do; ours was a *bustiko*, a linen bra-like garment. It was the *sayo*, a long sleeveless brocade dress with a rich floral design that was so elegant and impressive. All of these layers were covered by an apron or *devantal*."

Grandma remembered her *kapetana*, a short waist-length jacket, lined with fur worn over the entire ensemble. "It was part of my trousseau," she recalled. "I lost all of my beautiful outfits in the fire."

"*La kofya*, a headpiece worn by the women of Salonica, was very complicated," she explained, "and they were very fussy about how it should sit on their head!" The *kofya* consisted of a small linen cap with a brocaded snood. "I would insert her long heavy braid into the hat, keeping the whole thing in place with two decorative cords," she said. "Then, over these layers I would add a piece of velvet covered with seed pearls and lace. Some people even asked for a red ribbon to encircle the entire headdress."

Pearl necklaces, in single or many strands, were an essential part of the costume, and for those who could afford it, *una mannia de oro*, a bracelet of braided strips of gold, or a chain, *una cadena de oro*, enriched the outfit.

By the turn of the century, young women were beginning to wear Parisian clothing, although some elderly women
continued to wear the elaborate outfits on special occasions
until the outbreak of World War II.

Mom, born at the turn of the century and influenced by
schooling at the French L'Alliance Israelite, was glad to be
relieved of the complexities of traditions which burdened
women with costly layers of expensive clothing. She gravitated
towards western dress, wearing simple dark skirts and white
blouses.

While Grandma worked diligently at her business, her
family watched the years go by with no promising suitor on
the horizon.

It was an early spring in the late 1890s, when the Jewish
community held its annual picnic. The air was clear and the
brilliant sun highlighted the plastered facades, the red tiled
roofs and lush green of the cypress trees. As Rachel Benrube
took a head of lettuce to rinse clean in a cold stream, Jacob
Saltiel, a neighbor crept up behind her, touched her shoulder
and said softly, "I have been waiting for you for seven years."

"Why didn't you say so?" she answered quickly. Jacob,
a shy, tall, handsome, gentle and intelligent merchant was
looking for the right woman to be his wife. It was said that he
cared little for a sizable dowry and wanted no monetary
payment. Shy and cautious, he sought the right time to ask
this independent, exciting woman to share his life.

"The right man had finally found me and I hurriedly
worked to get a trousseau (*ashugar*) together with hand-
embroidered linens, summer and winter bedspreads and
curtains, which I tucked into a cedar chest and an imposing

armoire," said Grandma. "Like everyone else, we were married in a wedding attended by everyone in the community, without invitations but with much celebration."

The newlyweds rented a very large Mediterranean-style stucco apartment in *el cortijo* (the courtyard) and proceeded to establish a home. Like most of the old houses in Salonica, the plain whitewashed walls and shuttered windows presented an unassuming front. A large bay window or *shainishin*, which was often one half of the upper floor, protruded over the street.

"*Puediamos ver de tres lados*," she said, describing the unobstructed view on three sides as a stream of humanity passed their window. Many of the small houses were set askew with courtyards draped with honeysuckle. On some streets facing bays almost touched creating narrow shadowed passageways.

"One huge room was set aside for the business," she remembered, another, *el verandado* served as a big living room, a place to welcome guests who sat on the divans covered with woven spreads. *Los dulces*, the sweets, were set out on the round pedestal table in the center of the room.

Papa adored Grandma and deferred to her wisdom, allowing her to rule the home, an atypical practice for a man of his time. "*Lo que dice Rahel*," whatever Rachel says, was his answer to many questions. Grandma referred to him as "*papa, el buen djithio*," the good Jew. However, during the early years of their marriage, when in the Turkish tradition women rarely appeared in the market place, it was up to Papa to choose meat and select the daily supply of fruits and vegetables from the marketplace.

19

Jacob was not devout but observed Jewish high holy days. He worshipped in *un kal* (a synagogue) called *"Figo Loco"* (the crazy fig), a humorous name for the Synagogue Catalan Yashan in Salonica, which dated back to the 1500s. The name Saltiel can be found in Catalan synagogues, in Synagogue Shalom and in the Romaniote synagogue Ets-ha-Haim. In all there were 36 different synagogues in Salonica, and whether secular or religious, the Jewish population would greet each other on the sabbath with *"Shabat, shalom."*

The Jews in each courtyard shared a communal table, a house of worship and tended to celebrate away from the eyes of the Christian community lest they arouse old animosities. Some people believed Jews were slaughtering a Christian child at Passover seders when they referred to the "blood of the lambs" during the service. Since expulsion from Spain, Jews were very wary how their traditions were interpreted.

It was around their synagogues that Sephardi held their schools, libraries and organizations to care for the sick, the poor and the dead. Each community had a unique character.

Rachel's brother Avram married Delicia who bore him 15 children, but only eight survived the plagues of childhood. Tia Delicia's image and the experiences of her children were brought to life almost daily in our home.

There were the sons, Moshon, Jacob, Baruch, Pepo and Salamon; the daughters were Matilda, Julia and Miriam (Marie).

Rachel and Jacob added their two daughters, Marguerite and Julie, to the generation of children that lived together in a compound, saw each other daily, teased, played, struggled and rejoiced.

Mom and Grandma often told us about our second cousins in Europe. "Baruch, *era un hombre fuerto, un hama* (a strong man, a longshoreman)," recalled Mom. "We all had fun with Pepo, *un jugeton* (a clown) was always pulling tricks on someone. But it was Julia, Avram and Delicia's oldest daughter, *un poco fea pero gorda y fuerte, con un corazon grande*, a little homely, overweight and strong, who was loving and remains my favorite. I miss them all."

Tio Avram Benrube was the leader of a group of porters who worked on the docks in Salonica. While they intermingled with the indigenous Greek population, the Jews of Salonica didn't intermarry but shared similar traits such as thrift, respect for women and devotion to family.

The city of Salonica had seen many public disasters. It had suffered a thousand calamities: plagues, cholera, a widespread fire and other contagious diseases in addition to the tragedies of natural disasters and wars. It was common for people to resort to superstition in their fight for life and the safety of their children.

As Tia Bona lost infants from diarrhea or typhus, my grandmother prayed that her Marguerite and Julie would survive childhood.

Among the Sephardim, an amulet (gold hand with five engraved fingers suspended from a small chain pinned to an infant's cradle,) was meant to guard against *el ojo* (the evil eye) and especially *aynara no* (evil should not befall us).

These traditions extended throughout the Sephardic culture in other parts of the Mediterranean. My sister Essie recalls that "when daddy was sick as an infant and had convulsions, the family called in a rabbi who wrapped some

21

small objects in a handkerchief. The handkerchief and its contents remained hidden under his pillow throughout his life. When we eventually opened the cloth packet, the only item we could identify was a piece of parchment."

The Jews of Salonica were panic stricken when the Turks withdrew and the Greek army entered the city in 1912-13, but they didn't take flight en masse. They appealed to leading Jews and organizations in Europe to prevent annexation by the Greeks and to maintain Turkish rule. If it wasn't possible, could Salonica become an international city and a free port? There was no real intervention. The Allied Powers only interfered when the Bulgarians and Greeks approached Constantinople and forced an Armistice.

Destruction of the Jewish quarter of Salonica by fire, and the deepening fracture in this great community which faced serious economic and political difficulties under Greek rule, eventually resulted in the migration of thousands of Jews to Turkey, Europe and the Americas.

Nazis decimated a pre-World War II Jewish population of 60,000 Jews to the 1,000 which remain in Salonica today, and Sephardim remain the majority of the 6000 Jews that reside throughout Greece.

Daily Life In Salonica

"*Que ermosura era Salonique* (what a beautiful city it was)," recalled Mom. "The narrow streets of Salonica and the promenade along the quay were noisy with peddlers. *Estaba llenos* (full) of men and women *en el charshir* (marketplace), some strolling, others marketing, all carrying *un saco* (a cloth sack) holding daily purchases.

"The city, surrounded by domes of ancient churches, had a skyline pierced by 70 minarets, echoing a melancholy chant for prayer."

Allahu ekber, Allahu ekber,

La'illah ill' Allah

In *el charshir* small stalls held burlap bags, overflowing with rice, grains, beans, brown lentils, green split peas, nuts and firm chick peas. Here shepherds from the hills came to sell their lambs and crossed paths with tinware merchants and cloth vendors. "*Pan caliente* (round loaves of fresh hot bread) were tucked under my arms and bunches of vegetables strung on raffia dangled from my wrists," she related.

The covered bazaar with dozens of shops featuring silks and cottons, the air fragrant with the intense smell of powdery spices was in microcosm the spirit of the community.

The Salonica harbor about 1915.
Courtesy of Robert Bedford, The Foundation for the Advancement of Sephardic Studies and Culture.

Street vendors hawked, and *hamales* (bearers) unloaded ships amid the hustle and bustle of a seaport that brought excitement and adventure to Jews in a city at the crossroads of two continents.

"The Jewish quarter which rose above a bowl-shaped hill was a series of tightly packed compounds of wood frame homes, *casas hechos de laja*, which looked down upon the harbor," said Mom. From the top of the hill the city appeared as a mosaic of red/brown roofs and dark green cypresses. In the distance was the shimmering waters of the gulf, Thermaikos Kolpos (an arm of the Aegean Sea), and on the horizon snow-capped Mount Olympus.

Ever since the capture of Salonica by the Turks in 1430, the Moslems had lived on the slopes of *Chaoush Monastir*, the

The city of Salonica about 1916 as it rose above the harbor.

hill overlooking the sea. When the Spanish Jews arrived in 1492, they settled in the quarter between the sea wall and the street of the Vardar, the Via Egnatia of the Romans which crossed the city from the Cassandra Gate on the East, to the Golden Gate on the west.

For hundreds of years the city was surrounded by ramparts erected by the Romans. As the city grew and changed, rings of stones that formed the ramparts were torn down. The broad quay along the waterfront was built on the rubble of the former sea wall. Finally, the eastern wall fell and was replaced by the *Hamidiye,* a wide tree-lined boulevard.

Few streets in Salonica had names and houses weren't numbered, but people found their way by landmarks based on events or significant buildings.

The old town of Salonica about 1910.

Djade de Veintem, the Avenue of 20, referred to a street 20 meters wide, *Utch Yomourta Mahalesi*, the Quarter of the Three Eggs, alluded to the bas-relief on a marble slab, or *Las Encantadas*, The Enchanted neighborhood, site of the caryatids, erected by the Romans but later removed to the Louvre in Paris.

La Torre Blanca, the white tower also known as *Beyaz Kulle* was the centerpiece of the city, its image impressed in my mother's mind throughout her life.

The Tower, a defensive structure, dated to the 15th century. Later it was used as quarters for the Janissaries (soldiers in the elite Turkish guard) and as a prison for those who were sentenced to death. It was built on a site where an older Byzantine tower created by artisans under Murad II once stood. This Byzantine turret connected the east wall of the fortification of Salonica (the part preserved today) with the sea wall which was ultimately demolished in 1866.

26

The White Tower, a landmark of Salonica, as it appeared about 1910.

The Greeks in Salonica were largely clerks, small shopkeepers and manual laborers. The Turks, who were land-owners, and officials had little to do with the business life of the city. It was the Jews who became *hamales*, fishermen, fishmongers, firemen and peddlers of anything from cloth and brooms to fruits and nuts. If an odd-job had to be done, a hardworking reliable and honest Jew could be found to do it.

Often one could hear the thump of hot syrup being pounded into halvah in a wood-shuttered shop, or the wail of the milk vendor as he led his donkey laden with shiny goatskins through the narrow streets.

"As children we would follow on the heels of the Persian vendor who made beautiful arrangements of many colored sweets on a circular brass platter," said Mom.

27

Map showing Salonica, also known as Thessaloniki.
Credit: Alliance Israëlite Universelle.

"Julie used to watch *los zinganos* (gypsies) who worked as coppersmiths, tinning pots or large *basinas* used for soaking laundry.

"*No se pagaba lo que pedian* (we never paid what they asked), everybody haggled, quarreled and bargained. Not like here where you pay what is marked." For many years Mom couldn't get used to a single, listed price and managed to bargain effectively with Brooklyn merchants!

One of the significant characteristics of Jews in Salonica was the tendency to carry family traditions into business and trades. Since the majority of *hamales* were Jews, they organized into guilds, defined by where they worked and what they did.

The *hamal* in the neighborhood who carried coal was *il hamaliko do la kioshe*, the *hameles* of the streams who handled oil and leather were *los hamales de los choricos. Los ratones* (rats) carried, assembled and disassembled heavy machinery; *los hamales de la stacion* worked the railroad station, and *los hamales del commerco* were the stevedores at the port.

With a large tray and a hand scale, an energetic person had the hardware to start a business in the city. Peddlers meandered through the neighborhoods calling out their wares. Fruit vendors often added *pepitas de melon y pepitas de calabaza* (melon and pumpkin seeds) to their stock of citrus fruits. One favored vendor hawked *pistil*, a dried leathery-looking apricot paste. Broom sellers, cigarette peddlers and cloth merchants wore their inventory on their back, waist or in their arms. Often these trades passed on from father to son.

Of all the Jewish communities of the Diaspora, there were fishermen only in Salonica, where they enjoyed this freedom. Spanish exiles to other areas of the Mediterranean faced more restrictive employment.

The *Moros*, deep sea fishermen, were away for a week at a time, while the *Gripari* fished shallow waters. Both had their own guilds with constitutional rules, providing in detail for the social welfare and security of their members.

After anti-semitic incidents on June 30, 1931, many of these *hamales* emigrated to Haifa in Israel where they manned the city's port. Today the Spanish-Jewish idiom of Salonica can be heard along that city's quay.

Our family thrived in a community that respected the work ethic and gave each laborer space and security to survive with his skills, ingenuity, strength or the sweat of his brow.

My Papa Jacob, formerly a well-respected grain merchant, couldn't find a job when the family settled in Brooklyn. He immediately crafted a glass enclosed candy cart and sold sweets at noontime to local children outside of public schools. Work, any work, was dignified.

One winter afternoon in the 1940s, as we all gathered around the table for a lunch of *fijon y arroz* (beans and rice), we chatted about the special presents offered to our then president Franklin D. Roosevelt by heads of state.

"Ah, those are all rich people," said Mom, "but we weren't.

"In the early 1900s, when a visit from the Sultan of the Ottoman Empire was expected in Salonica, the elders of our community met to talk about this important occasion. Remember, we lived in peace with the Turks and Greeks but wanted to offer a gift to the Sultan to insure his favor."

The city erected triumphal arches, flags were draped on the buildings and sand covered the cobblestones to smooth his carriage ride.

"What were we but a community of exiles," she explained. "All we had was what was secretly taken when we fled from Spain. *Despues de tanto tiempo todo era nada mas que unos handrajos*, after 400 years, our treasures were little more than a few tattered things, all that was left of our glory in the lands of our ancestors.

"No one knows if the grand rabbi of Salonica or a poor bedraggled woman made the offering, but when the great one appeared, someone carried a ragged bundle to the Sultan. *Imahinate. En los trapos abia un gayina de oro con dies poyitos,* just picture the whole thing. The rags covered a gold chicken and 10 gold chicks, all seated on a gold tray. This was indeed a present suitable for a sultan!"

When Mom's grandson James Russell traveled to Salonica in 1975, he wrote to his parents, Charlotte and Joe, describing his experience in detail. The Sephardic *Home News* printed excerpts of his letters:

> I am writing to you from the great Rotunda. The light and air here are most beautiful. I am getting used to the sunny chaos of Greek political life, the ridiculous, amidst extraordinary antiquities and the fragrance of lilacs.
>
> I have found the synagogue and the Jewish community center. Yesterday I climbed the walls high above the harbor and looked at old deserted mosques. The mosques reminded me of the Sephardic past. Just now a fragrance appeared in the air, a spice Grandma used, I think....
>
> The city is good for walking at night, and everyone does. There is music....
>
> Outside the window a dove is cooing, and a drawn Byzantine chant echoes through the court. It is a sunny cool day. I have just finished a lunch of *matza, taramosalata* (fish salad), olives and fresh fish I bought at the market. It was splendid, but I do miss all of you, especially on *Pesach* (Passover).
>
> Yesterday evening at seven, I went to *shul* (synagogue) and was given a seat up at the *Aron Kodesh* (Ark)

31

near the Chief Rabbi Shabtai and the president of the community, Mr. Perahia.

The service was exceptionally beautiful even though there were only 15 or 20 people in the *shul* (synagogue). The chanting was very much like what I imagined the music of Salonica to be.

Then I walked with the Rabbi to his apartment on the Corniche. His wife died, but a Sephardic woman, a neighbor who had survived a concentration camp, cooks for him and takes care of his house.

She was there with him and another woman, a relative from Istanbul, and his niece Margarita, who is about my age, 21.

The *matza* on the seder plate was *matza shemura*, or a special super kosher *matza*; round, unleavened cakes, about an inch thick and four inches in diameter. We began to chant the *Haggadah* (the book containing the ritual of the Seder and the story of the Exodus) in Hebrew.

The Rabbi read in *Ladino* from an old book in Hebrew script, I read in English, Margarita read in Greek, and when the Rabbi shouted, "Turkish," the lady from Istanbul would read in *Ladino*.

The *Pesach* (Passover) wine was specially bottled kosher in Athens and we drank each of the four cups from big water glasses.

Sure enough, there on the seder plate was the *charoset* (a mixture of apples, figs, apricots, spices and honey to represent the texture of the mortar used to build the Pharoh's temple), the *maror*, a kind of endive used in Salonica as a bitter herb (to represent the bitter life suffered by the Jews) and three pieces of the *matza*.

When we got to the part before the meal, he bellowed, YO-KHOLOO-HOO, and I remember Mom always said that was when you were supposed to dig in.

Then we had boiled eggs, spinach pie cooked with *feta* cheese, anchovies, olives, cucumbers, tomatoes, a special dish of lamb and peas and some *raki* (anisette). Servings of fruit and nuts was followed by a meringue and cream for dessert.

Significance of the bath house → gossip

It was almost midnight when the women left to go home, but I remained with the Rabbi and sang songs *Echad Mi Yyodea, Chad Gadya, and Ki Lo Naeh Ki Lo Yaehm,* the way Dad does. He was pleased that I was half Ashkenazic as well as half Sephardic, because he said that made me entirely Jewish.

After that, we talked and he showed me pictures of the dedication of the Holocaust memorial, at which he officiated with representatives of the Greek and Israeli governments, and a picture of his wife who had passed away. The Rabbi told me to stay in Greece and get married here.... It was some *Pesach*!

Jimmy closed his recollections by describing Salonica as "the city of Perahias, Saltiels, Ben Rubys, Shabatis, Molhos and Behars, the Aegean and the sun of Greece. *Shalom m'Salonik.*"

ENTERTAINMENT

Djoha stories permeated conversations for centuries in Salonica and continued to underline our expressions when we wanted to emphasize a moral, a word of advice, or to add a sense of humor to common everyday occurrences.

A single expression embodies the departure of Ladino from Spanish as well as an inkling into the lifestyle of the period.

For example, "*Djoha se fue al banyo, tuvo do kontar mil y un anyo.*" (Djoha went to the bath house and found enough to talk about for a thousand and one years.)

This quip reflects the importance of the bathhouse as a social and hygienic experience, a place for men and women to catch up on local gossip.

Marguerite and Julie heard about *Djoha* as a "cunning rogue, trickster, prankster, loafer and joker." This *azno* (ass) was not originally a Jewish character but was known as *Juja*, a popular figure in Arabic folklore.

During a peaceful period, before the clouds of war had gathered over Salonica, some sophisticated residents of the city were enjoying the "cinematograph," introduced by the French. At the turn of the century there were privileged showings at the cafe of the Hotel Columbo in the French quarter. "Some said it was a magic lantern," said Mom, "with people who appeared alive moving through a story."

The hotel set up marble-topped tables in the viewing room where people enjoyed refreshments and played games like backgammon and dominoes as they waited for the show to begin. Vendors circulated with small bags of pistachio nuts, and children were treated to sugary lemonade.

Before the magical event, moviegoers saw a live show that often featured a singer, a magician or a contortionist. When the white sheet was lowered and fastened, and gaslights dimmed, the featured attraction appeared. On screen, images of men and women appeared, took up various positions, smoked cigarettes, ate and fell into deep slumber; the audience was stunned.

Ten years later the cinema regularly showed the latest films of the Vitagraph Company, and on occasion Papa took Marguerite and Julie to see this marvelous entertainment.

By the time the family settled in New York, movies were an accepted entertainment for the masses. The whole family loved the cinema and recalled the wonder and celebration with the arrival of "moving pictures" in Salonica.

L'ALLIANCE ISRAELITE

While education at home was largely devoted to lessons from the past, Marguerite and Julie were among the fortunate young women to have an opportunity for an enlightened education at L'Alliance.

From early childhood Mom was recognized by the family as bright and gifted, learning to read and write at an early age. Up until her late 80s, she served as the scribe for many families in Brooklyn who needed help corresponding with friends and family in Europe.

At the close of the 19th century, the energy put into establishing commerce and industry in Salonica spread to the founding of schools.

Each community, regardless of its ethnic identity, relied on educational programs to express their particular philosophy and their independence from schools in other communities, as well as from the Turkish state itself. There was the German Gymnasium, Le Petit Lycee and the schools of the Lazarist Brothers among others.

The Alliance Israëlite Universelle (AIU) with headquarters in Paris was a major factor in educational reform. The driving force of community leaders and scholars such as Dr. Moise Allatini, Joseph Nehama and Rabbi Jacob Meir resulted in the establishment of a primary school in 1873

35

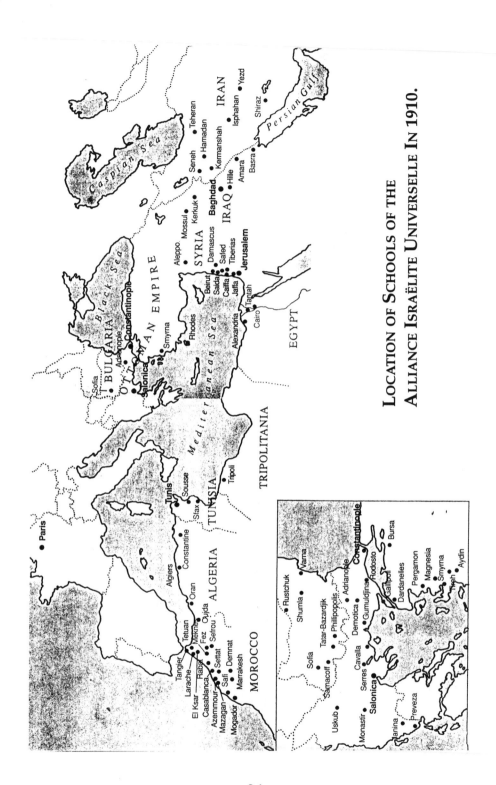

LOCATION OF SCHOOLS OF THE
ALLIANCE ISRAËLITE UNIVERSELLE IN 1910.

36

which grew to a network of nine schools in Salonica by the time Mom was 12 years old.

The organization, begun in Tetuan, Morocco in 1862, expanded to include 127 schools throughout the Mediterranean area by 1939, with over 47,700 students. Today, schools which use materials developed by the Alliance's *Creer Didactique* can be found in Belgium, Canada, France, Hungary, Israel, Morocco and Spain.

By 1909, over 12 percent of the Jewish population had been influenced by the Alliance. Almost anyone who was successful in commerce, industry, medicine or the legal profession credited AIU with launching their education.

AIU is recognized as the most important institution to bring regeneration to the Jews of the Mediterranean. Consciously or unconsciously, the founders were agents of cultural imperialism for France. Wherever the Alliance created schools, the major language of instruction was French. Spanish was never taught at the AIU in Salonica and families relied on Ladino. My father's education at the Alliance in Tetuan included instruction in classical Spanish in addition to French.

It was at L'Alliance that my mother learned flawless French, received an education that prepared her for a career as a journalist and gained an awareness of the potential for a new life in another land.

Sephardic teachers trained in Paris taught ideas developed in Western civilization and were educated in moral training which transformed concepts of life in the Orient. Mom came to know the culture of Victor Hugo and the spirit of *Liberte, Egalite and Fraternite*. Moral self respect was inculcated

37

through more knowledge, better appearance, better manners and less clannishness, as education raised the horizons of both boys and girls, encouraging an understanding of other religions and denominations.

It follows that Mom, who absorbed culture like a sponge, was so strongly influenced by the Western ideals taught during her school years that her adjustment to the democratic principles in America easily fit into her outlook on life. Throughout our childhood this avid Francophile would quote words of wisdom and summaries of the works of great French writers like Moliere and Racine. *Marseillese*, the French national anthem, was sung in our kitchen as often as the American national anthem, and the *tricolore* (French flag) always waved in her memory.

The Alliance sought to export its talented students to other areas of the Mediterranean to teach in its schools and bring the West to the East.

What was particularly significant about this militantly westernizing teaching corps is that it was made up principally of Middle Eastern and North African Jews trained by the Alliance in Paris, who came back to spread their adopted culture with all the zeal of the newly converted. The Alliance teachers constituted one of the first westernized indigenous elites among the Jews in the lands of Islam.

When the family migrated to Koritsa (Korice) in Albania after the 1917 fire in Salonica, Mom taught school in a rural mountain village. Julie also taught although she had attended a Catholic school in Salonica. A rambunctious student, she was unwelcome at L'Alliance.

In spite of the ideals professed by AIU, the differences

among teachers and their attitudes affected my mother's education. "The rich students got preference over those who were poorer," she recalled. "Your Grandma burned the midnight oil sewing school uniforms for me; she wanted me to be one of the best, but in those days the wealthy were favored."

Nevertheless, her scholarship prevailed and a future for advanced study in Paris was on the horizon as World War I broke out. "I actually missed a boat departing for France, and once the war was on, I stayed at home and got a job."

For Mom, her first job as a reporter remained as one of the most important achievements of her life. "No Jewish woman had ever applied for such a professional job," she told us. "But I did and I proved myself."

At *L'Independent* the vivacious, eager young woman with fire in her eyes and thick hair as dark as night met people of culture and fell in love with Alberto Alchek, the newspaper's young, handsome editor who treated her as an equal. The idealists talked for long hours, edited each other's work and dreamed of a future together, unhampered by matchmakers, traditions and *el ashugar* (trousseaus).

Unfortunately, custom prevailed. "I knew he was too much to hope for and I wasn't surprised when he revealed that with too many sisters to marry off, he couldn't marry me," she often said wistfully.

Mom always made it a point to see movies starring Dana Andrews. "Ah, Dana Andrews, *me encanta* (enchants me). With his dark eyes and manly features, he was so handsome, just like Alberto," who served as a fantasy as remote as living a lifetime with a matinee idol. After marriage to my father, a prosperous American at that time, she made a point of sending news to Alberto, bragging that she had married well in the new country. Yet we all knew that she held the flame of that first love for most of her life.

The French press in Salonica represented the most respected journalism of the time and gained popularity with Sephardim in Salonica and other areas. *L'Independent* endured until the Nazis shut it down in 1941.

War

Although caught between many conflicting cultures, Salonica, nevertheless, moved towards modernization by the late 19th century.

Tangled Balkan wars starting in 1856, which later involved French and Germans in 1870, Russians and Turks in 1877, and Greeks and Turks in 1897, transformed the city into a center for military operations and gave rise to unprecedented economic revival.

Historian Joseph Nehama describes this period in which foreigners, tourists and merchants streamed into Salonica. The harbor was alive with ships of all nations. Consulates sprung up as prosperity fostered a sense of economic well-being. By the time Mom was born in 1900, the city had become part of the European railway network. The new century saw radical changes, as streets were widened and gas lights introduced along with a new water supply system. Electric trams began to thread their way through the city's streets in 1907.

Where did the money come from? International and local Jewish financiers were responsible for leading Salonica into the 20th century. Hirsch, the Rothschilds, Allatinis, Modianos, Beys and Kapandjis were among the names of those who invested in early industries. New landmarks rose around the city as seven of the ten largest industries which included mills, a brewery, brickworks and textile factories were funded by Jewish businessmen.

A financial crash in 1911 and the unification of Salonica with the Greek state led to the relocation of major Jewish industrialists, the merging of their companies or take-overs by Greek businessmen.

In spite of the crash this commercial center featured banks, insurance companies, brokerage houses, printing, publishing and shipping enterprises. Hotels, large stores, cinemas and increasing cultural institutions attested to the driving force of Jewish influence.

MACEDONIA

Macedonia, described as a brewing cauldron of discontent, was a tragic corridor crossed by people on the move, always reaching for freedom. Bulgarians, Greeks, Vlachs, Albanians and Turks separated by mountains and hemmed in by valleys were distinct and aloof from each other, clinging to age-old customs and traditions.

In 1893 a few men assembled secretly in Salonica, the gem of Macedonia, to plan for the liberation of the people from the tyranny of Turkey. They fervently believed that an end with horror is better than no end at all, and came together with IMRO, the Internal Macedonian Revolutionary Organization, an underground force.

The Turks, who did not distinguish among trouble-makers, burned villages and massacred residents. While storms gathered, life in Salonica kept its usual pace as the city was in Macedonia but not of it. The Bulgarian population, the most fervent of the freedom fighters, believed in action.

In 1903 reprisals for Imro's guerrilla (*cometadjis*) warfare brought Salonica out of a state of complacency as bombs exploded and cavalry stormed through the city in the wake of the explosion of the steamer *Guadalquivir*, bound for Constantinople.

Local activity escalated behind the shuttered doors of shops, and hiding places were created. Underground tunnels dug under the commercial area of the city were charged with nitroglycerine.

As bombs exploded, burying the sites of the German Club, local banks and schools, the city was thrown into a panic. Fehmi Pasha, the governor, took to the streets quieting people and the haranguing mobs. In spite of the death and destruction, Europe did not intervene but only sought to protect its nationals.

BALKAN WARS

Before the onslaught of WWI there were two tangled Balkan wars in 1912-13. When the Great War broke out, the Balkan nations found themselves battling the same enemies they had recently fought. One needs a a score card to unravel the web of allies and foes; and once calculated, the powers then shift once again.

The first Balkan war in October, 1912 occurred when Montenegro declared war on Turkey. It was later joined by Bulgaria, Serbia and Greece who were eager to seize the Turks' remaining European territories.

While Turkey was defeated, the allied countries immediately quarreled as the Serbs wanted Salonica and a larger share of Macedonia from Bulgaria. The Greeks wanted the same territories. In June, 1913, Bulgaria attacked Serbia and Greece. Montenegro, Romania and Turkey joined the Serbs and Greeks, and Bulgaria was defeated.

In WW I the Serbians, Montenegrans, Romanians and Greeks joined the Allies and their former enemies Bulgaria and Turkey joined the Central Powers. By 1914 the Balkan lands were an unfortunate pivot of world history.

The recent collapse of the former Yugoslavia, which was formed to "solve" some of the problems described, clearly suggests that little has changed as these poor areas continue to be vulnerable to international and domestic politics and confrontations.

My ancestors didn't come from a village whose traditions and culture were static, unaffected by change. More than any single area in the world, Salonica was in the center of infighting between ethnic minorities, while at the same time on the cutting edge of Balkan industrial and cultural awareness.

Jewish voices affected policy, Jewish newspapers took a stand and reported worldwide news, and Jewish men and women were immersed in international events. One wonders what would have happened to our families had Salonica been spared by the fire that ravaged its core, or if Hitler hadn't destroyed those brave souls who sought to keep the roots that took hold four centuries after expulsion from Spain.

After the second Balkan war in August, 1913 and in accordance with the Treaty of Bucharest, Salonica was annexed to the Greek State.

Moreover, it secured the approval of the Great Powers for the final annexation of the city to Greece and quelled some of the foreign propaganda which exploited the anxiety of the Jewish community.

The Turkish character of the city rapidly changed. The wealthier Turkish families fled when the Greeks took over and the distinctive red fez disappeared. Arabic characters no long decorated shop fronts and posters as Greek ones took their place. In Byzantine churches holy icons displaced *suras* of the Koran which proclaimed the oneness of God.

With the outbreak of the war, 300,000 soldiers of the Entente entered Salonica by October, 1915, creating a strategic stronghold for the Eastern Campaign under General Maurice Sarrail. The influx resulted in increased business opportunities for the Saloniklis.

For Marguerite, a bright, energetic young woman, the war, its soldiers, sophisticated foreigners and hubbub brought excitement to *L'Indépendent* and gave her a chance to spread her wings, an escape from the drudgery common to women. She covered stories and established connections which were instrumental to the survival of her family. It was her words, her slant and her ideas that appeared on the front pages of *L'Indépendent*, the newspaper hawked by newsboys on every street corner.

From a logistical point of view Salonica was an inadequate Greek port with only a single track rail line running north to Bulgaria. Historians view the Allies' belief that it was a tactical stronghold as one of the war's mysteries.

To make matters worse, the countryside was described as terribly unhealthy, malaria ridden, subject to heavy flooding in winter and intense heat in summer. As the situation deteriorated in the Eastern Campaign, the position at Salonica was called the Allies' largest concentration camp, as the army was occupied fighting disease while swelling in numbers at the same time. By 1917 it consisted of a force of 600,000 men, mainly French and British but with Serbian, Italian and Montenegrin contingents. Its only accomplishment was to keep the small Bulgar Army from breaking out somewhere, although in reality it had no where to go.

In retrospect, Salonica was without a doubt the most ponderous, illogical undertaking of World War I, but even its irrelevance did not gain public attention.

During WW1 the Jews fought as Greeks and were so treated. Based on this relationship, Greek political and military leadership refused to consider discrimination against their co-citizen Israelites.

As a result of the Peace Treaty of Versailles after WW I, Salonica was given to Greece. This decision increased the Jewish population in Greece to 125,000 with an estimated 60,000 in Salonica. During the period the city was under the aegis of Turkey, there was rioting in the streets between Jews and Greeks, which continued after the Greek government took control.

These provocative acts were not accidental. The Greek Nationalist Movement, initiated by Prime Minister Venizelos, proclaimed, "Greece for the Greeks," even though Jews had been living there for 2000 years. Among their early acts of oppression was the destruction of Jewish cemeteries and later the ban of their headgear, the fez or tarboush.

In 1923, when Mom and her family had settled in America, 160,000 ethnic Greeks transferred to the city from the Turkish mainland, and the rise of conflicts in business and trades further impoverished the Jewish community. By the outbreak of WW II Jews were steadily emigrating to the United States, Latin America, Palestine and France. Some even considered returning to Spain after 400 years in exile.

Today, Greece is a country where 95 percent of the population is Orthodox Christian. Not only had Salonica never commemorated its more than 50,000 Holocaust victims, but there were few references in school textbooks to the richness of the city's multicultural past.

Of the 36 synagogues that thrived in the Jewish quarter, only one remains. The city has been slow to recognize that its large and vibrant Jewish population was singled out for annihilation. The silence has finally ended. In the spring of 1997, the year when Salonica, Greece's second largest city, celebrated its turn as the European Union's cultural capital, a memorial to the Holocaust victims and two museums dedicated to Jewish life and culture opened to the public.

Fire destroyed the Jewish quarters in 1917. Courtesy of Robert Bedford, The Foundation for the Advancement of Sephardic Studies and Culture.

THE FIRE

The fire was the turning point in the long history of the family's life in Greece. 400 years after their flight from Spain, they had emerged as a strong culture in Salonica, only to become wandering Jews once again.

But, adversity sometimes offers opportunity. What would have happened to Marguerite's daughters if we were raised in Greece. Would we have emerged as independent women or, like our relatives, become one of the 46,000 deported Greek Jews who faced unimaginable brutality at Auschwitz and perished in Hitler's ovens?

"I'll never forget the date, August 18, 1917 (*lo tengo en el meyoyo*); "it's forever in my mind. It was the day when the Great Fire of Salonica almost totally destroyed our Jewish community."

During the Macedonian Campaign in the First World War, when Salonica's population grew fourfold, swollen with thousands of British, French, Serbian, Italian, Russian and Greek soldiers, the city was more susceptible than ever to fires and plagues.

In 1990, when I purchased a new house, Mom asked, "Is your house made of brick?" When I told her it was made of red cedar, she wasn't pleased. "*Hecho de laja*," she moaned. "Wood is no good. What if it caught fire? Then you would have nothing."

The flames that changed her life never completely died down, flaring up over the course of 70 years to fuel old fears. "The old town, the Jewish quarter where we all lived, was crowded," she said. It would only take a few strong gusts of the feared "Vardar" wind to start a conflagration similar to fires which destroyed portions of the town in 1890 and later in 1910.

New York historian and filmmaker Robert Bedford, whose grandmother emigrated from Salonica, conducted an in-depth study of the fire and its survivors, describing the disaster which affected the future of thousands of people.

Under occupation, the ancient city with a population of 150,000 in 1914, had now reached 300,000. Salonica's reputed squalor, eastern way of life, narrow streets, overhanging porches, narrow wooden buildings and intense heat made life miserable for the occupying British and French. The city was ripe for disaster.

On a stifling Saturday afternoon in August, the fire began in a little wooden house on Rue Olympias in the Mevlevihane quarter. The pan in which a refugee woman was frying eggplants overturned, the oil caught fire and from there the flames spread.

It was the Sabbath, and Jewish firemen with antiquated equipment could not respond immediately. By the time the city was notified by two cannon shots, the fire fanned by the strong Vardar wind that had been blowing hard for two days reached alarming proportions. "The Yedi Kule was a standard form of alarm, a leftover from the days of Ottoman occupation. The number of cannon shots indicated the location of the fire," writes Bedford. "In the older Turkish days it was the *Pasvan*, the night watchman patrolling the city who would sound the alarm in case of fire."

The Vardar was really a fearsome force of nature. According to the accounts described in many interviews with survivors, the wind was responsible for carrying the fire throughout the city.

On street after street, carts pulled the belongings of people driven out of their homes. Panic was building. Refugees piled featherbeds on their backs, carting treasured useful as well as useless items from their home. Every family tried to save their sewing machine.

As confusion reigned, the French military began to dynamite in an effort to create a "breach," a common practice in halting the spread of fire. But, the strong wind and inflammable conditions couldn't prevent the fire from leaping over any breaks. To make matters worse, the roar of dynamite led people to believe that they were under attack.

The fire spread, Allied armies tried to help and the British ran hoses with the benefit of modern fire fighting equipment from their navy vessels docked near the sea wall. Raging out of control, the fire changed direction, ultimately destroying the wooden bazaar.

Hamales (bearers) as well as private cabs and carriages were called, but in the ensuing chaos it was impossible to find anyone, and nearly everything was hand carried.

"Help us save our belongings," screamed the refugees, as the fire tore through their city, while smoke blackened the sky and their world crashed at their feet.

"Julie and I couldn't hold Grandma as she ran back into the house," said Mom. "Like dozens of others, she was desperate to recover the treasures that took so long to acquire." In a society where the few items owned were cherished forever and passed down through generations, a trousseau was meant to last a lifetime, and risks were taken to save it.

"Her heel got stuck on a ledge while she raced through the apartment that was choked with smoke and flames. She tumbled forward, crashed into smoldering boards and broke her hip. Papa dragged her out of the building before she became engulfed by the flames. It was a nightmare."

Grandma was treated for a few days at a French Army hospital which had a women's section. The French had taken over the Jewish Hirsch Hospital and established a few others.

As hysteria subsided, the little family gathered in shock to find shelter and survive. What now, where were they to go? As the armies sought refuge for men, women and children, rushing them to safety on the Monastir Road, my family rushed to the grain warehouse, where luckily, as a supervisor, Grandpa Jacob could find safety for his family and injured wife.

At night they heard the scratching of rats larger than cats scuttling through the ominous building, gnawing at sacks of wheat.

However, as grain holes enlarged, the family nestled in the corner of the cavernous warehouse was showered with falling grain. "As the grain poured like rain all around us, I got an idea. Why waste it?" she said. "I started to put handfuls of grain into bags made from ripped up pieces of cloth and sold the small sacks for a few cents to refugees seeking food."

Martialing assertiveness acquired as a journalist, Mom stepped out of the warehouse and snaked her way through the fire ravaged streets, making deals with local people for fresh water, while Jacob and Julie tended to Grandma as she lay in pain on a hard pallet.

The hubbub of life in the quarter came to a halt after the fire. The busy crowded streets with vendors' carts that had clattered over the cobblestones and the buzz of mingling crowds were gone, as this ancient, thriving and glorious Jewish community of the Near East was decimated.

According to Bedford, the loss of the local synagogues and their contents which included torah scrolls, historic manuscripts, libraries and treasures carried from medieval Spain severed Salonica's ties to the past, for each was the stronghold of some particular community whose members originally came from Seville, Granada, Toledo or Aragon.

To make matters worse, the community was stunned by the loss of almost all of the historical features which the distinctive Jewish presence had imprinted on Salonica over the centuries. Although actual destruction covered little more than a mile and a quarter of the central city, it demolished institutions that were part of the life blood of the Jewish sector.

Photographs of the city before and after the fire reveal skeletons of buildings, ragged remnants of brick walls and stark smokestacks.

Casualties were light in Salonica. The fire was so methodical in its approach, so consuming, that it was easy to spot and easy to realize it was headed your way. "Everyone just grabbed their stuff and fled," added Mom. "Since it lasted for days, people ran away from the danger but faced death elsewhere. The problem was where to put 73,000 homeless people; 52,000 of them were Jews.

The fire, and the bombardment to extinguish it ordered by General Sarrail of the occupying army, caused the destruction of 4000 buildings, more than half of which belonged to Jews who then found themselves homeless and helpless.

The allied forces and Red Cross provided food. Although there were attempts to provide secure shelter for the refugees, many wound up in tent camps and hospitals. Packed together in small rooms, dark cellars, stables and sheds with little hope of permanent housing, the mortality rate rose to ten times the normal.

General Maurice Sarrail, the leading general in command of the Expeditionary force, was not well liked. He was stationed in Salonica for political reasons, since his supporters in France lobbied for his commission. Despised by the Jewish community, he was often in contention with the British and Italian forces as well as his own. Immediately after the fire, he was recalled to France.

Life changed dramatically when the troops left Salonica. Much of the military possessions were given back. Barracks and newly built structures were sold to the Jewish community since the government did nothing to help them find housing. Neighborhoods were organized around these structures (the Campbell section which experienced anti-Semitic incidents in 1930 was a community built after the fire) and they endured extreme poverty and uncertainty up until the Second World War.

Almost 1000 of the poorest people fled to the Aktche-Mesdjid district, a miserable area rife with rubbish and pestilence.

During the war the soldiers had provided a fair amount of wealth for merchants and shop owners. With their departure, the Jewish sector was left at the mercy of the Venizelos government, and many Jews eventually fled to seek a new life elsewhere, settling in Paris, Palestine or across the ocean in America.

Politics once again reared its ugly head. It appears that the Greek government had decided on a policy of Hellenization which would once and for all establish their ethnic claim to Macedonia. This was effected at the expense of the Jewish community who saw little change in their situation. Christ. anti-Sem.

In 1922 the Turkish victory in Asia Minor caused nearly half a million Greeks to leave Turkish territory and settle in Greece, many to Salonica. Jews who were once the majority, became the minority. A city that was once determined by them had been changed literally and figuratively, as the Greek Christian population tripled.

The Macedonian and Greek refugees who settled in Salonica were anti-Semitic, and were responsible for the fascist and anti-Semitic riots and incidents in the 20s and 30s. This period also produced the Sunday Laws, the special Jewish electorate and many other measures, which despite their intent worsened the Jewish standard of living.

After the fire, at the urging of the French military who knew Marguerite as a journalist, my mother and her family left under cover of darkness for Kuricea (Koritsa) in the mountainous regions of Albania close to the Greek border. Why? Was she a courier carrying important messages across the border?

"We know that she had information to pass on and was serving as an envoy, but she kept the secret locked within her," said Essie. "While she told us all she could about her past, she never revealed the messages she bore during one of the most dramatic events of her life."

In Kuricea the family lived with local farmers and survived on the meager earnings Mom and Julie earned teaching in a rural school.

It isn't hard to imagine Mom organizing everyone, caring for Grandma with a broken leg and dragging the family's paltry belongings to an unknown area where few Jews existed. Essie still has the *Yambole*, a red Turkish wool shag blanket stored among the family heirlooms. It was part of my grandmother's dowry that traveled from Salonica to Koricea and finally to America, covering her frail body till the time of her death in 1962.

IMMIGRATION

What would it be like to leave a homeland, a language, a people? Marguerite had secretly pored over maps of the United States of America in the small offices of *L'Indépendent*. She looked at photos of blue lakes, towering mountains and vast green plains, recalling impressions of this melting pot from the few films she had seen.

There was no home left after the fire, people were slowly scattering to all corners of the world, disease was spreading. The family had to get out of the hostile environment for Jews in Kuricea. Who was to take the first step and make the decision to emigrate?

While the Turkish Empire was collapsing, steamship companies doing business with the United States were sending agents to the Near East to recruit passengers.

Marguerite read the accounts of merchants and dealers who had visited America during expositions. She heard about the coffee houses like those in Salonica that offered a place for men to socialize and carry on business deals. Photographs of American women unharnessed from suffocating corsets arm-in-arm with tall attractive men strolling down New York's Broadway captured her imagination. More importantly she read about the movement to allow women to vote.

Tia Bonna, Grandma's sister, was already living in New York City on the Upper East Side. Letters related dramatic changes in the life of Bonna and her children, Regina and Alberto, but often ended with a sigh of homesickness. Nevertheless, the family was prospering, and a connection was established. It was up to Mom to reach out, make further arrangements and plan for the voyage.

Marie, Tia Delicia and Tio Avram's daughter, asked to join the family of four emigrants and was a "sister" for Julie and Marguerite till the day she died.

With a mixture of excitement, anticipation and a little sadness, the homeless family left behind their beloved city, never again to see the ancient ramparts, the sparkling gulf or hear the wail from towering minarets.

When they boarded the *Patris* in the port of Pireaus a short distance from Athens, little did they know that this hulk was to make its last transoceanic voyage and would be transformed into scrap soon after docking in New York Harbor.

Grandma sold her diamond earrings to pay the $45 passage for each member of the family. Their scanty luggage consisted of little more than the few things carried on their backs in the frantic escape from the fire.

The *Patris* pitched, yawed and creaked for 20 days. Seasickness was rampant. Immigrants packed into steerage slept on tiers of steel beds with paper thin straw mattresses. Stacked five high and three across in cramped, poorly ventilated quarters, the human stench of vomit, body odor and waste was enough to make those who didn't have sea legs nauseous. Many like Grandma suffered fierce cramps, rumbling bowels and dry heaves.

58

The incessant noise of the anchor chain, the turning screws, people packed like sardines babbling in a dozen tongues and dialects, babies crying and the uncertainties of admission into the land they hoped would transform their meager existence, was enough to wear out and wear down the most stalwart.

"The food was so awful, and we didn't even know what was in some of the soups," said Mom. "We appealed to a steward for help or Grandma would have starved and were grateful when he gave us a bags of stale bread and a sack of raw onions. Papa, Marie and Julie, who was recovering from typhus ate little more than Grandma."

Sometimes when the seas were calmer and the night clear, Marguerite would climb to the deck for a breath of fresh air. Removing the black scarf which covered her head, she would then loosen the thick braid, allowing her hair to catch the breeze.

"One night I looked up and saw a shower of stars with a brilliance so intense it could swallow the world," she recalled. "I wasn't afraid. As I lifted my eyes to the heavens I saw it as a good luck sign. One of the sailors told me it was the Northern Lights and, 'wasn't I lucky,' since it was the first time he had ever seen it in all of his journeys.

"Would we be one of the 12 million immigrants to be welcomed by the lady in the harbor? I was standing at the bow of the ship and saw the colossus slowly emerge. The Statue of Liberty was overwhelming, her bright torch held high, but she had a benevolent face. She was a woman like me, strong and brave in any storm."

The whole family was detained on arrival because Grandma was crippled from the hip fracture sustained while escaping the fire. At Mom's insistence, Le Croix Rouge (the Red Cross) had issued a letter indicating that the injury was not caused by disease and would pose no health threat. Also, Grandma, an accomplished dressmaker, could contribute to the family income.

"We worried day and night," she said. "What if we were all sent back to Greece because of me. We had sold everything; there was nothing left."

ELLIS ISLAND - CASTLE GARDEN

The huge cavernous halls held hundreds of immigrants clinging to their pathetic bundles, all in fear of some aspect of the examination. Sick? They would have to go back. No bond posted? Goodbye. Girls expecting to meet prospective bridegrooms were jilted? Board the next ship. Fear more than disease was contagious as immigrants dreaded the scrutiny of keen-eyed inspectors.

In gloomy noisy hallways, standing in endless lines for examinations, they waited anxiously. Where is the promised land? Julie had a nosebleed. "Cover your face before they see you," urged Marie. "Don't complain!"

Each morning the family left a comfortable bed and sat at a table set for breakfast with stewed prunes, hot cereal, fresh bread, butter, jam and a stack of hard boiled eggs. Throughout the day social service workers from the Milk Fund, sponsored by Mrs. William Randolph Hearst, walked among the huddled groups calling loudly, "Fresh milk for babies!"

To Marguerite there was no doubt, they had made the right decision. It was only the beginning, but she sensed that

America would fulfill her promise to immigrants. Wasn't it obvious how rich the country was? Food was plentiful, light bulbs shone, toilets flushed; there was an abundance of soap and hot water poured out from shiny, brass taps.

Jacob, Rachel, Marguerite, Julie and Marie lined up at trestle tables for endless interviews, as officials filled huge ledgers with information, "Do you have job waiting for you? Who is your sponsor?" They waited for the coveted landing card to welcome them to America. Finally, the stamp of approval to land lifted their spirits, as Ellis Island turned out to be an Isle of Hope, not an Isle of Tears.

Tia Bonna, accompanied by her daughter Regina, Regina's husband Prosper and her son Alberto, reached out her arms to grasp her sister. Bonna took the weary travelers to her apartment, a tenement on 106th Street and Park Avenue.

"We left it all behind," recalled Mom: the war torn burned out city, the hand-to-mouth existence, the rigid class structure, the filth and the pestilence. The family began a new life, as the front door to freedom was held open.

But, they had also left a strong extended family, a culture that had become refined over the centuries as well as familiar traditions, institutions and customs. The Saltiels were among the 60,000 Sephardim that eventually settled in a few major American cities, another stop in the great Diaspora that reached back to Salonica, Seville and the holy lands of the Bible.

SALTIEL/SANANES FAMILIES

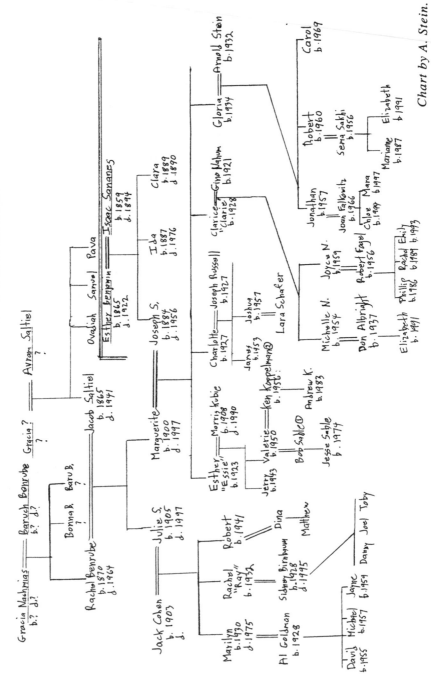

Chart by A. Stein.

62

New York, New York

When the Saltiels arrived in New York City in 1919 they were following the path taken by millions of immigrants from southern Europe entering a different world on the cutting edge of change.

The small family stepped on American soil as the seeds of the women's movement were taking root. The 19th amendment had been approved giving voting rights to women after a long hard battle by the suffragettes.

Warren Harding was in the White House and the first transcontinental phone calls were connecting America to the world. "Abie's Irish Rose" was a hit on a Broadway lit by neon signs.

Americans faced their first 1040 tax form which levied 1% on $20,000, 6% on 500,000 and above.

Hems were raised above the knee midway through Calvin Coolidge's administration, and stockings were rolled down during this age of sheiks and shebas, when no-waistline dresses meant that the days of tight corsets were numbered.

"I wondered why people needed closets full of clothes," said Mom. "In Salonica we were satisfied with *un vestido para las pascuas* (a holiday outfit), a few dresses for visiting and serviceable older clothing for housework. When one wore out, it was replaced. No one worried about being seen in the same thing twice!"

A new vocabulary filtered into the language of those who were "hip." Guys, who could "cut the mustard," carried a torch for a gal who was the "bees knees" in spite of her "cheaters" as they all piled into "jalopies." The new lingo presented an additional challenge for the greenhorns who were struggling with basics.

Bonna had sponsored the family which quickly found a home on Park Avenue and 106th Street. Other immigrant families lived in the building and before long the three young women met an American girl who lived across the narrow, dark hall. Goldie shared their joys and their sorrows, often leading them by the hand as they explored their corner of the city. The concept of "girlfriends" was unfamiliar in Salonica, where the Sephardic community maintained strong family ties and was suspicious of strangers.

It was exciting, frightening and often overwhelming for the immigrants who leap-frogged into the tumult of 20th-century America. The steady pulse of the city and the fresh outlook of the intermingling masses inspired Mom's youthful spirit as she broke free of the decaying traditions of Europe with old rivalries, doubts and fears.

The huge buildings were taller and grander than the minarets of Salonica, and the streets held a sea of humanity. As elevated trains resounded overhead, the cavernous subways swallowed up millions of New Yorkers in suffocating rush hours. Sometimes Grandma would wonder, *"que is esta locura"* (what is this madness), but she knew it had been a good move and the best one they could have taken.

The Roaring Twenties were the Gatsby days of tightly fitted cloches, prohibition, bootleg gin, and a reign of gangster terror while jazz rang out from dozens of night spots reaching up to Harlem. The Saltiels gathered around a neighbor's table radio, learning about daily events and the adventures of fearless men recklessly performing airplane stunts. "It was free entertainment," recalls Mom, who had never been to a concert hall or a dance.

Modern medicine was raising life expectancy to 54 years and people didn't perish from the kinds of pestilence found in the "old country" where a high infant mortality rate was a fact of life. *Los primeros son caballeros* expressed the feeling that often the first child died young.

Hollywood fanned the flames of a world where anything was possible, as the matinee idols fulfilled fantasies. On screen Rudolph Valentino and Ramon Navarro were the quintessential Latin lovers. Joan Crawford in slinky gowns danced her way into the imagination of Marguerite, Julie and Marie.

Julie swooned over the images of tall, dark and handsome actors on the silver screen. In spite of limited English, the whole family went to the movies where they could watch Ruby Keeler and Dick Powell looking larger than life, tapping their way to happily ever after on 42nd Street. This was America, where all dreams came true.

"*Imaginatodas las escuelas eran de baldes* (imagine, all schools were free, even for adults and foreigners)," explained Mom. Julie, Marguerite and Marie immediately enrolled in night school as a major step towards assimilation. Although Mom didn't describe her experiences in the classroom, she must have learned very quickly since she eventually wrote and spoke English with ease, translated for other immigrants and took care of everyone's correspondence.

"Marie was always absent from night school," she recalled. "I would trick her by giving her the wrong words to say and we would all have a good laugh." Within a few years everyone except my grandmother who was house bound learned and functioned in English, a testament to perseverance.

Citizenship was acquired as soon as possible, with no regrets. The family never had any intention of returning to Salonica; this was their home now, their new language and they were immersed in the mainstream of New York City life as soon as possible.

It wasn't until the 1940s that Grandma achieved her dream of becoming an American citizen. Charlotte took on the responsibility of tutoring her in English and the basics of American government.

In the 1960s, when I taught new waves of immigrants to speak, read and write in English at an evening school program in Manhattan, I often thought of my mother. *The Education of Hymie Kaplan,* which was written in the mid 1920s, formed a basis for my humanistic approach to the curriculum and my students.

In recalling incidents of the early 1920s in New York City, Mom said, "I could only find factory work at first. One boss offered a salary and on pay day, I found less in my envelope. *Me engano,* he cheated me, thinking I was just an immigrant and should be glad to get what I could. I quit and looked for another job."

Mom and Marie got jobs embroidering beaded dresses

with a "Mrs. Stockholm." Periodically they had to attach a cord to a heavy bundle of garments, drag it onto the subway and deliver the order to a customer.

> **Mom**: It was on one of these trips that a man approached me in the subway car, pinched my arm and ran off the train at the next stop. I showed him! I left the bundle with Marie, got off the train, followed him up the stairs from the station platform and gave him a big pinch *en su culo gordo*, his fat behind. I shouted at him in broken English "Don't touch me" as I refused to let him get away with it.

After surviving war, misfortune and fire, this spirited 20-year-old woman was ready to take on subway flashers and molesters. On a separate occasion when another lecher tried to grab her buttocks in a crowded car during the rush hour, she was prepared. "I now carried a hat pin in my pocketbook, in case and stabbed him very close to his private parts, where I was sure it would leave a memorable scar. Wasn't I learning fast?"

In describing some of these early experiences often accompanied with peals of laughter, we were taught an early lesson in defense and dignity. As a result we became resilient, less fearful or traumatized by the kinds of incidents that confronted us on many subsequent subway adventures.

MARRIAGE

> *El cazo es un regalo, el parir es un mal paso, el crear mas todo el ano.* (Marriage is a gift, birth a passing pain and children an ache for a whole year!)

Clarie: It was in the tradition of Jewish families in Salonica and other Mediterranean countries to provide a suitable dowry for their daughter. It was a constant preoccupation when a female was born. In some parts of the world things have never changed, and for millions of people in China today, baby girls are considered dispensable.

Males brought wealth to a family, females depleted it and matchmakers generally arranged marriages related to social standing and size of the family treasury. In Salonica, dowries and trousseaus were appraised by professionals. This indication of wealth was displayed on the wedding day at a parade through the streets of the Jewish quarter, as the couple wended their way to a new home.

When the dowry of Tia Pava (Grandpa's sister) was appraised, the evaluator complained that it was excessive for a bride from her background and could set a precedent that would cause hardship to families of equal standing who had to compete. Aren't today's excessive celebrations of weddings and bar mitzvahs reminiscent of keeping up with the community till debt us do part?

Good families with limited dowries made less desirable marriages. Since young women often died in childbirth, the only hope for a spinster or poor girl was to marry a widower and take on a ready-made family.

My mother's whole world was turned topsy-turvy when the fire destroyed all they owned and threatened her dowry and her future. She couldn't marry Alberto Alcheck, *un hombre de meyoyo* (a man with a brain) and the love of her life. Alberto had unmarried sisters to provide for and it was expected that he fund their dowry before thinking of his own future.

Although the rigid mores of the Orient had relaxed over the years, allowing for some contact with the opposite sex, the web of tradition continued to trap young people and their dreams.

Alberto hoped Marguerite would wait for him. "Why are you leaving," he asked when she told him she was migrating to America.

"Because there is nothing for me here any longer," she answered, hoping he would plead with her, but he couldn't.

When she married Joseph Sananes, Mom sent Alberto a copy of the wedding photo, her dark eyes glowing as she wore the latest flapper-style silk wedding dress, a beaded headband enhanced with pearls and high heeled white satin shoes; a large bouquet of roses cascaded from her arms. Her new husband, prosperous in a formal tuxedo stood at her side.

> **Clarie**: Although she had taken colossal steps in trying to achieve a measure of independence in Salonica, the tradition of dowries and male superiority was part of the fabric of her life, as she mixed with the immigrant community in New York.

Tia Bonna had a son, Alberto, who was considered an idiot and not marriageable to girls with a significant dowry. Bonna cast her eyes on Marguerite. She knew the family; her niece was good looking, reliable and strong, more importantly, didn't have a cent.

"*Yo no iba casar con un bovo con stivaletos*, I would never marry anyone who was real dumb or annoying *como un primo hermano de la pesgadia* (a first cousin to a pest!)," said Mom, "and my mother and father stood by me."

69

Yes, Rachel was grateful to her sister Bonna for all the assistance in providing a refuge in New York, but the answer was a definite, "NO." Alberto definitely didn't "cut the mustard."

The rejection caused a lifelong rift between Bonna and Rachel, one that never mended. Old attitudes die hard. Although they were all strangers in a new land and the sisters needed each other more than ever, bitterness prevailed as Bonna *chaba cuerdras para pelear* (threw out a rope for arguments). The contention between my grandmother and her sister was to be repeated between Julie and Marguerite.

Potential bridegrooms were plentiful in the 1920s as thousands of men who had emigrated sought European brides. It was important for the family to form a union which carried on Sephardic traditions and to avoid *la basha ropa* (low class people). While romance was a remote bonus, earning a living and providing for a family was the prime consideration. Then as now, power and money served as an aphrodisiac for women all over the world.

Suitors came and went from the little tenement apartment on Park Avenue as Marguerite searched for a suitable husband. Often, the scene was full of comic elements. When funny-looking girls found handsome husbands, they would remark, *se namoro Montezuma de un culo de pepino* (Montezuma fell in love with someone who looks like the ass-end of a cucumber).

As matchmakers arrived with promising bridegrooms in tow, Julie was positioned at a rickety table that furnished the living room.

"One of the legs was shorter than the others," recalled Mom. "It was Julie's job to hold up the table while a possible future husband was visiting."

A book was placed on the wobbly table as a lure. If the suitor held it upside down or had little interest in its contents, he automatically failed the test. *"Me paricia un bovo y no valia, y meyoyo no se mete con cuchara"* (he was too dumb; not for me, after all, you can't feed someone brains with a spoon).

Avram Alcher made it to the starting gate but was taken out of the running when on a stroll down Park Avenue, arm in arm with the beautiful Marguerite, he met a widower. "I offer my congratulations," said Avram. *"otro asno, another dope,"* said Mom. "Even I, a greenhorn, knew the word should have been 'condolences.'"

Boyfriend number two, Alberto Moro, who was educated and more compatible with Marguerite's ideals, almost made it to the finish line. Proud of Mama, he took her to meet his landlady who promptly asked, "So, Albert, how are the children?"

"What children?" asked Mom.

"I didn't tell you?" he said. "I have two, a boy and a girl. But don't worry, they're boarding with a family."

"I was wary of this man from that moment," said Mom. "The fact that he concealed the children from me made me think he had too many secrets."

Enter another matchmaker with another winner.

"I have a perfect gentleman for you," said Reuben, the smiling marriage broker. "He's handsome, intelligent and rich. You're sure to be happy with this one. Few men have so many fine qualities."

Wedding photograph of Marguerite Saltiel and Joseph Sananes, 1922.

Once again the family dressed for the visit, took out a tray of *dulces y rosquitas* (sweets and biscuits) and awaited perfection. As soon as the bell rang, Julie was positioned at the table, and the book was in place.

"When the door swung open I saw Reuben, but where was the match?" thought Mom. "I looked up, then I looked down. There he was, a midget, right next to the greedy matchmaker. He might have had all of the other qualifications, but I cringed, *mucho bashico*, too short. Not for me."

Finally, the trail of matchmakers and potential husbands ended when Bonna's son-in-law Prosper acted as an intermediary and introduced my future father to my mother.

Joseph Sananes turned the book right side up and could even read it in English. At 5'4" he was somewhat shorter than Mom and had a slight limp as a result of childhood polio, but he was a good looking man. Although he was 15 years her senior, he was educated, intelligent and ran a successful business. Dad's generosity played no small part in her decision to make him her husband and she hoped for the best. *Dame un grano de mazal, y echame a la mar* (give me grain of good luck and then throw me to the sea).

All four of us eventually were thoroughly schooled in the dangers of matrimony. *La engano* (he tricked her) was drummed into us from the time we could listen in on adult conversations. If a woman became pregnant out of wedlock, there was only one reason, she was fooled by male lust, and if the marriage took place at all, it was doomed to failure. The idea of females craving sex or enjoying an affair was out of the question, and a "fallen woman" only had a man to blame.

73

Mom would often sing a droll song of a faithless husband and spurned wife.

Morishco mi alma
porque vienes tarde?
El hijo esta yorando,
que quiere ver al padre.

Yo no quiero al hijo
ni te quiero a ti
arrematate de aqui.
Yo quiero a Estrelina
de noche y de dia.

Morris, my love,
Why are you late?
Your son is crying
And wants to see his father.

I don't care about my son,
And I don't care about you either.
Get outta here!
I love Estrelina
Day and night.

JOSEPH SANANES

My father, Joseph Sananes, was born in Tetuan, Morocco in 1884 to Isaac Sananes and Esther Benjamin. The family emigrated to the United States when Joseph was an infant and settled in what is now the Bath Beach area of Brooklyn. Esther had a daughter Ida (Veda) shortly thereafter and a daughter Clara who died during infancy.

Isaac, for some unexplained reason, was known locally in Brooklyn as "Frank." A sometimes politician, our grandfather is believed to have buried a nest egg to finance a home for his family and to bankroll his own trip to Alaska in search of gold.

> **Clarie**: Esther Benjamin had no great love for Isaac, an attractive man with bright eyes, a classic Roman profile and wavy, reddish-brown hair.
>
> In Morocco she had loved *un pepitero* (street vendor selling pumpkin seeds), but her more middle class family wouldn't allow it. Since it was her turn to marry, she settled for Isaac who was approved by her parents.
>
> Isaac's brothers were businessmen living in South America. A self-educated man, Isaac was involved in New York City politics. We never knew exactly what he did, but there was some indication that he had some shady dealings that remains a mystery to this day.

The family collapsed when Isaac died of a sudden heart attack in 1906, at the age of 36. No one knew where he had stashed the cash that was supposed to fulfill the family's dreams. His death left behind a penniless, bitter wife, a 12-year-old son and a pale, repressed daughter. Esther lived for a short time with her sister Messaude in Brooklyn. Although she was well educated in Hebrew, she was unable to care for her children in America, and the fatherless family returned to Morocco.

My father, who spoke flawless, unaccented English, also studied at L'Alliance in Tetuan where he learned Castillian Spanish along with French; Ladino was never his language of choice. He and Mom would often have heated debates about the meaning or origins of words. He spoke flawless, unaccented English.

Dad read the daily *New York Times*, among other newspapers, was a Republican and believed in the freedom of the small business man unrestricted by government. When Franklin Delano Roosevelt was heralded as the greatest president—Dad flew in the face of popular opinion and voted for Republican John Dewey in 1944.

When it came to politics, my parents were sharply divided. Mom believed all men were created equal—Dad, some more than others, especially if they were white and had money.

While he belonged to the Morocco Society of America, Joseph had little in common with Moroccan Jewish men who held to Middle Eastern attitudes towards women. His desire for a son was no secret, but he appreciated his daughters and insisted on expanding their educational horizons. Matchmakers, early marriages and lifelong careers as homemakers belonged in the lives left in Greece and Morocco. He was always proud of our accomplishments.

The small wedding in 1922, only one year after her arrival, had an air of simple elegance. Joseph bought Marguerite the formal wedding dress and threw a reception for the family and a few neighbors. He also bought his mother Esther and sister Ida clothing for the affair, but his mother refused to attend.

Clarie: She was a nasty, bitter woman. Having lost a dashing husband when she was still in her thirties, she never married again. Esther was unwilling to give up her 37-year-old son to another woman.

It was on a two-day honeymoon to Philadelphia that Mom had the first chance to be away from the security of her family. This trip did not whet her appetite to see the world. "I had seen some of the old world and I didn't like it," she often said. "Philadelphia was okay, but New York is the greatest city on earth."

Mom and Dad settled into a small apartment near Grandma on upper Park Avenue. Romance was relegated to her imagination as she prepared to face the reality of her role as a wife. While she respected my father, she never mixed it up with love. And, as for sex—well, it came with marriage and had to be endured. She often spoke to us of Alberto Alchek, the only one who ever captured her heart and seemed to be the theme of the *romanzas* (songs of love) that she frequently crooned. I would like to think that she held on to the love of her life in her dreams.

Quien hijo cria, oro hila (To rear a child is to spin gold).

One year after the wedding, Ethel (Essie) was born and named after her paternal grandmother. What a joyous occasion it was for an older bachelor and his immigrant bride when their first child was born on American soil.

Clarie: While Mama and Daddy craved a son, he wasn't disappointed with the birth of a daughter. I still believe that the birth of a son in the family would have overshadowed all of us.

77

After Essie's birth in 1923, the couple bought a small house in Brighton Beach only three blocks from the ocean; it was Mom's first home of her own.

My father, as was typical of the time, brought his widowed mother and sister to live with them. Even while Esther was alive, the two witches, made Mom's life a hell and before Essie was born, Dad moved them out to an apartment.

> **Clarie**: When Esther Sananes died at the age of 56 of a heart attack, my aunt Ida, a pale, nasty, repressed and angry stereotypical spinster came to live us. She stepped softly, with a cheshire grin on her face, never laughing aloud, always planting seeds of discontent. Mom suffered in silence, but Dad knew there was trouble in the household. When it became obvious, he once again had to move his sister to her own apartment nearby.

Ida had a nasty disposition and harbored a well developed fantasy life, believing no man to be good enough for her. She often carried a picture of the dashing matinee idol John Bowles in her handbag, imagining that someday someone like him would come to call.

In 1926, without telling his wife, Dad bought a beautiful, relatively new, completely furnished, two-family, semi-detached brick home on a tree-lined street in the up and coming Bensonhurst area of Brooklyn. Joseph Sananes presented the deed to his young wife. "The house is in your name," he said.

An affluent husband, a new home and a beautiful baby; everything was happening so quickly. Maybe the streets were really paved with gold and opportunity in America.

Good Times—Hard Times

Boca dulce abre puertas de hierro.
Kind words open iron gates.

Until Charlotte was born in 1927, little Essie, an adorable round faced, pudgy child with deep brown eyes was treated like royalty by a doting grandmother, young aunt and the newlyweds. Wrapped in a fur coat, fur hat with matching blanket in winter, and draped in frilly dresses in spring, she was a joy to behold. A gold bracelet encircled her small wrist and a color tinted portrait of the beautiful toddler hung in the family's living room.

Charlotte, the spitting image of Mom was the second much loved and welcomed child, as the household brightened with beautiful little girls. Unexpectedly Mom became pregnant again, and Clarice was born in 1928. The red-headed Clarie with porcelain white skin was to emerge as the family artist.

There was always room for one more as Dad prospered, dealing in furs, dabbling in real estate and taking risks in a soaring stock market.

Charlotte: When we first moved into the downstairs apartment on 66th Street in 1926, Grandma lived a few blocks away near 18th Avenue in a tiny house

79

heated by a coal stove. Later she moved to a railroad flat on 20th Avenue between 64th and 65th Streets over an "appetizing" (delicatessen) store.

Our apartment on 66th Street had beautiful textured wallpaper in the hall and on the porch. It was there that I first heard President Franklin D. Roosevelt proclaim during the Depression that "we had nothing to fear, but fear itself."

At this time Julie married Jack Cohen, an orphan from Safi, Morocco, who had jumped ship in New York harbor. Marie married another *Marroquino*, James Abisror, and now the three young women had established their families.

> **Clarie**: When we lived on the first floor of the two-family house, the second floor was rented to a dentist and his wife who had a Swedish maid, Helen Petersen. Helen and Mom became life-long friends, sharing recipes, stories and a love of children.

Mom always said, *No hay mejor espejo que un amigo viejo* (There is no better mirror than an old friend).

The life of Jim and Helen Petersen and their twins, Vera and Frank, were followed through the years. When Helen moved to New Jersey the women corresponded regularly and exchanged cards, as we heard about life in "The Garden State," and the milestones reached by the children.

Vera married four times, often led a trailer park existence and lived in Alaska among many other places. Frank wasn't successful with his marriages either. In spite of many heartaches, including the suicide of a grandchild, the parents loved each other for over 60 years.

The Petersens' relationship represented an ideal for Mom. Jim, a hard working, good natured, honest, lean and handsome man, was a loving father and husband. He turned his paycheck over to a sweet, smiling, pretty, capable, blonde, blue-eyed wife, who wore a crisp house dress topped by a clean bib apron. Helen didn't shriek, whine or nag, as they raised well behaved, adorable children.

They were a 1930s version of "Leave It To Beaver," but quite real and unchanged through the years. Nevertheless, our friends weathered many storms as their children emerged from the snug, loving cocoon to face less than ideal circumstances in their own relationships.

When the dentist, Dr. Beller, and his family moved out of the two-story home, our family moved to the second floor, and Julie, her husband Jack and our Grandparents moved into the ground floor apartment. The family had come together once again in a mini-compound, like *el cortijo*.

The family had no hint of the impending disaster in October, 1929, that was to change their lives along with millions of other Americans, when the "lack of more margin" was the straw that broke the back of the Big Bull Market and signaled the end of Coolidge-Hoover prosperity.

A major part of the family's capital was invested in stocks. On "Black Friday" Dad lost everything but our home and a few near useless investments. Within a few days, Mom, who had struggled most of her life, was back counting pennies to keep her family off the bread line.

> **Clarie**: I think Mom was more accustomed to adversity than luxury. During the "good years" she maintained a simple life and wasn't comfortable with

affluence. Gifts of powder, perfume, jewelry and expensive garments which Dad showered on his young wife often wound up in Julie's dresser.

The crash left my father humbled, confused, despondent and suicidal, as he lost everything that raised him from the slums of Morocco. At the age of 45 he could barely put food on the table for his growing family.

Rising each morning at the usual time, Dad would resume his routine of going to work at a job that barely existed; the routine was the only shred of dignity he had left. Grandma watched her son-in-law pick at his food, often withdrawing to rest in a dark room.

Grandma, who could turn a phrase in any emergency, called her son-in-law into her room. "Sit down," she said calmly, as she took his hand in hers. "What did you have when you were born?"

"Nothing," he answered.

"Yet you survived and took care of your mother and sister when your father died. What did you have when you returned to America from a youth spent in Argentina?"

"Almost nothing," he answered respectfully as his mother-in-law looked him in the eye.

"Pull yourself together," she urged. *"No es muerte de gente,* (no one has died). *Estas desnudo otra vez* (you are naked once again). You succeeded once; you are a good man who has taken care of my daughter and grandchildren. I believe in you. I trust that you will triumph once more and take care of your family."

Dad kissed his mother-in-law's hand and left the small room.

For Mom, a totally selfless woman who professed an interest in socialism, the crash returned her to a position of reliance on her ingenuity, as she felt a kinship with those who had no roof over their heads.

While the family never returned to the comfortable halcyon days of the 20s, they did progress and flourish. Rachel Saltiel had a mesmerizing way with words. My father revered age and wisdom, and his mother-in-law gave him back his dignity with the same sense of confidence that empowered hundreds of people who came to her in search of the strength beneath the surface of their lives. She did not merely offer lip service, but was present every day to guide her children and their families through the trials of marriage, and the difficulty of raising children during hard times.

The Depression sapped the hearts and souls of people everywhere. But, we had a roof over our heads, taxes were paid and magically we ate well with minimal resources.

When the crash came it brought home the harsh reality that in the end, money is only printed paper. Once again my parents had to endure, building on the will, strength and courage that brought them to this country. The loveless marriage no longer was sweetened with any fringe benefits; nevertheless, the family had to prevail and move on.

One of the best things about my father was that he was so predictable. His predictability offered security and a safe way to behave with a volatile personality. We always knew what pleased him and what bothered him, as we were warned to rarely approach him with a problem.

After the initial shock of reduced circumstance lessened, Dad was frequently impossibly nervous with children around him and Mom would send us to another room. We ate at 4 p.m. daily, giggling and talking. He ate at 5 p.m. sharp, without watching children play with their food or interrupt his peace.

Current perspectives on family dynamics might suggest group meetings, compromise and negotiation so the family could communicate more effectively. But Mom instinctively knew better. Dad was set in his ways, and ultimately with her understanding, peace reigned.

Joe Sananes was rigid, consistently rejecting change and refusing to do anything differently under new circumstances. She was a liberal Democrat; he was a Republican. Now, poor once more, he still believed in capitalism, while she found solace in novels that affirmed her belief that the poor will inherit the earth as a reward for their suffering. Rags to riches was the dream for both, but tinted with a different hue.

An unexpected pregnancy in 1934 after numerous miscarriages left Mom tired and frail. At 34, her hands were rough and swollen, the result of scrubbing with harsh laundry soap. Her drawn, thin face, decaying teeth and thinning hair made her look ten years older. How could she raise another child, with a husband who was 50 years old and a budget that seemed too tight to stretch any further.

One afternoon in the late 1940s, as we sat on the porch recalling the old days, she remembered the night I was born.

> **Mom**: When I entered Kings County Hospital the night I went into labor, I felt something special about this birth, and hoped for a boy, a special gift for your father. After you were born, I awoke in a private room,

84

and the nurse handed me another sweet baby girl wrapped in a pink blanket.

But, what was I doing in the lap of luxury in the midst of the Depression when I was admitted as a clinic patient? Was it a mistake, would we have to pay for something I didn't need, and was this my baby?

"There were no beds left in the ward and we had to place you here," smiled an attendant, "but don't worry, it won't cost you any extra."

My first breakfast tray arrived with a platter piled high with hot pancakes, a small pitcher of warm syrup, fresh squeezed orange juice and real cream for my coffee; I felt like a princess.

"What will you call the beautiful baby girl?" asked the nurse. I thought about it for quite a while. This clearly was a good luck child, even if it was my fourth daughter, and I would pick a name that would give her a good start in life.

"Gloria," I said. "I am naming her after Gloria Swanson, the movie star."

Naming me after a living, unrelated person was an unusual choice for an immigrant, Jewish woman. Traditionally, names were selected to honor relatives who had died. As an adult I emerged as the least traditional of the four daughters; Mom had indeed given me a special start.

Amor de madre, ni la nieve lo faze enfriar. (Not even ice can freeze a mother's love.) Once, angry at her for scolding me, I shouted, "If I died you would be happy. You never wanted me. With one less daughter in the family to marry off, you could enjoy the other three more."

Instead of getting hysterical at my obvious foolish behavior, Mom looked at me and said.,"Sit down." I knew a lesson was coming, as she always sought the teachable moment.

"How many fingers do I have?" she said, holding up four fingers. "These are my daughters. Do you think that if I cut one off, it wouldn't hurt?" I never forgot those words which I have repeated to my children and the children of others when they felt unappreciated.

As the youngest child, teased too often and on the fringe of the family core, it would have been easy for a tired, over-worked mother to ignore my presence. Through the years Mom applauded my good grades and achievements. I always knew that I could put a smile on her face with evidence of my good works; she instinctively felt that she had done well once again.

Instead of despair at having another girl, Dad threw a party in celebration of my birth. I often received special attention from both parents as I was offered the tenderest part of the chicken, spoon fed soft cooked eggs with bits of toast, and allowed to lick the sweet, fresh cream off the milk cap.

More than 60 years later, I cling to the story of my first day on earth in all of its embellishment, as well as the lesson on loving the runt of the litter. My unplanned arrival during hard times had some redeeming quality and indicated a bright future in the hands of a loving mother. Her caring and confidence in me served as a point of departure in my life, which has consistently focused on making each day worth living, taking occasional risks, figuratively "dancing on the table" in celebrations, seeking adventure and trying to fulfill my own dreams.

THE LEAN YEARS

Quina que nos cayo, manta que nos cuvijo. (Woe to us!)

It took President Herbert Hoover too long to admit that the nation had reached the end of its string when the U.S. banking system collapsed in 1933 and unemployment soared to 15 million, more than 25% of the population. My parents stretched the few dollars that arrived in the mail each month from some salvaged stock, and the pittance Dad returned home with each night from wholesaling cheap sweaters and perfume to street hustlers.

> **Mom:** The statistics didn't tell the story of swarms of pitiful men selling apples on street corners, or people waiting for a piece of stale bread and a bowl of watery, gray soup ladled out by charities.
> *El harto no cree al hambiento.* Those who had food to eat never felt the pangs of hunger of the poor, something I understood.

On many sleepless nights Mom worried, "What if?" What if Joe couldn't bring home enough pennies needed to make it from day to day? What if they found themselves homeless, with their possessions thrown onto the street like the nightmare of the last days in Salonica? What if they had to rely on the charity of others? *Seria que bethje estaba a la puerta*, was the cemetery knocking on the door?

As "Hoovervilles" dotted the American landscape and sprung up along the Hudson River and in Central Park, Mom, more than ever, clung to her home and the security it offered. The picture was bleak everywhere. Doctors and lawyers were making impressive $70 a week salaries, and a nurse could expect $15 a week if she could get a job. A lucky farm hand counted out four singles on his payday and a few sacks of food for the table. In our alley, unemployed men offered "small cash for old clothes" while beggars sang sad songs hoping to catch a few pennies flung from a window.

It didn't matter that you could get a small house in Brooklyn for $3000 or a 12-room villa for $17,000 in Westchester County. When you didn't have five cents for a pound of sugar or a loaf of bread, the bargains were meaningless.

> **Charlotte**: It was when we shopped with Mama and were included in deciding what to buy that we became aware of the stress of making ends meet. At the Italian bakery we scooped pastas with interesting shapes from wooden draws, and lightly burned our hands on the steaming bread pulled from huge, hot ovens, always weighing price and need.

In the 30s we had a limited income, no washer, refrigerator or accessible cheap entertainment. It would appear to have been the dark ages, but we relied for amusement on storytelling and movies told, retold and embellished. Afternoons were spent with family, neighbors or visitors, listening to tales from "the other side," or observing my grandmother and Mom solve the community's heartaches and problems.

We had few board games, no bicycles, roller skates or doll houses and relied on the radio, street life and holidays for amusement. When I was old enough to determine what I wanted, I would negotiate the day. I filled my hours with school, visits to the library, calling on a friend, listening to adult conversations, window shopping or taking a solitary walk under a bright sun or light drizzle to see another block, different people.

The six girls in both households made a big difference, sporadically entering each other's world of imaginary palaces and hideouts. We created pirate plunder and enacted mini-dramas in the recesses of the garage, the alley passage, the dimly lit basement or on the front stoop. Pick-up street games included ringalevio, stick ball, hide and seek, potsie, jacks, and any game that required equipment as sophisticated as a piece of chalk or a small ball.

"When we were given a few cents for spending money each day," said Clarie, "we immediately headed for the corner candy store to buy a piece of candy or a junk toy, 'made in Japan.'"

Months were marked by impending holidays, births, bar mitzvahs, weddings and bereavement at the loss of loved ones, while a white noise of family routines included school assignments, promotions, prizes, and the onset or outcome of childhood illnesses.

On slow, lazy summer days parents and children gathered on the front porch, cautiously leaning out the window to watch the passing parade. We could see who was dating, or who sported *un vestido a la moda* (an "up to the minute" outfit). We kept a running commentary on daily events on the block, deciphering Yiddish and Italian conversations, always vigilant as the street took care of its own, coming together at any sign of strangers or danger.

Solos were sung in the bathroom, but the musical chorus was held in the kitchen with everyone leaning over the ten-cent "song sheet" to get the words right. Songs like "Chattanooga Choo Choo," "Three Little Sisters," and "Amapola" were among the familiar tunes that spoke to us, songs that were heard a hundred times and harmonized with radio crooners.

> **Charlotte**: Most our singing in the kitchen was done while washing and drying dishes and before going to sleep. It was there that Mama sang "La Marseillaise" and declaimed Shakespeare and Racine in French.
>
> When Essie, Clarie and I were sleeping in the music room, an area adjacent to the porch where Grandma slept, we would croon, "I like bananas 'cause they have no bones," and recited "The Highwayman," by Alfred Noyes, in unison.

Everyone went to bed at the same time, 9 p.m., as night devoured day. During winter months hot water bottles warmed our space as we bundled up for cold nights under heavy blankets. Hot milk or cocoa before turning out the lights was mandated; instinctively Mom knew about the sleep-inducing effects of milk and it seemed to work.

Tired and worn, the furnace banked and secure in the knowledge that everyone was safe, Mom was the last to turn out the night light before going to sleep, knowing that tomorrow at dawn, as the sky gave up the light, the routine would begin once again.

Essie recalled living on day-olds from the A & P. "It was Charlotte's job to get to the store early on Monday to get the best of the Saturday leftover loaves at five cents a piece. It made great French toast for a big family."

We all remembered Dunkel's Grocery at the corner of

66th Street and 20th Avenue. Chubby Mrs. Dunkel could be found sitting on an old milk carton in front of the dark shop, munching on one of many meals she tucked into an old sour cream jar.

When the rich cream was removed from the milk, Old Man Dunkel sold the bluish, skim milk remains. We would take a glass quart container to be refilled with a ladle from a large can, and avoided the bottle deposit.

Mr. Dunkel, a tiny man whose rimless glasses were perched on a pointy, long nose, wore a battered brown fedora to cover his balding pate. In perpetual motion, he stocked the grocery's shelves to the ceiling and pulled down single items with long stick-pincers.

Up at 5 a.m., Dunkel would make home deliveries before opening the store, which supplied one of this and one of that on an as-needed basis.

A master of simple addition, the grocer would lick the tip of the well-worn pencil as he listed the item on the side of a brown bag, adding in Yiddish under his breath. When the lead began to blunt, he would whip out a knife and whittle off a few more shavings to sharpen the point.

During hard times few people filled a shopping cart, and too many had to put their meager purchases "in the book" till they could get some money, but Dunkel was rarely stiffed, as his customers were honest and understood his own struggle to make ends meet.

In 1933, it was President Franklin Delano Roosevelt who ushered in a new administration and a humanitarian approach to the nation's disaster. With an instinct for the common touch, Roosevelt sought to ease the pain of the Great

Depression with his "Fireside Chat" broadcast on the radio.

The New Deal, legislation which primed the pump of the pitiful poor, helped turn the tide toward a healthier economy with an alphabet soup of agencies: the CCC, PWA and the WPA among others.

> **Essie**: The holidays meant so much to us. Mama would wait for "dollar days" in the department stores and we would go to S. Klein on Herald Square where she would buy each of us a new dress. Dresses were two for one dollar and we would get new shoes for Passover and Rosh Hashonah. Fortunately, the $25 biannual check from Skelly Oil and Curtis Wright, leftover shares from the stock market crash, helped her give us what we needed, although it was meager.

> **Charlotte**: Momma loved to find bargains and we all had a turn at taking the subway to S. Klein. Clarie and I would crawl under the racks and play as she browsed. My favorite pair of "baby doll" shoes which I wore through college were bought for $1.50 at Orbachs.

I had "arrived," when at ten years of age, Mom agreed to take me shopping with her. She packed a few goodies for the subway, including some fresh orange slices, in case I got motion sickness.

As she rummaged through piles of shoes linked together with a string, or held her place as others pushed ahead reaching for special bargains, I quickly got tired of the adventure and wanted to head home. I still don't have the patience required to shop for clothes, and often pick up something in a hurry rather than flip through endless racks. Yet, Clarie and Essie still enjoy shopping and the pleasure of good buys.

Now, as I pass weekly yard sales in rural and suburban

Sign of assimilation
→ Christmas tree

neighborhoods, and watch consignment stores spring up everywhere with racks of clothing that groan under the weight of people's cast-offs, I think of the few closets we had for six people, and the ample space between the wire hangars.

Everything was handed down from one to the other until it was unwearable in public. Then it was recycled into night clothes, cleaning cloths or rags. There were no yard sales, since there was nothing to sell.

> **Charlotte**: We celebrated all the holidays including: Yom Kippur, Rosh Hashonah, Succoth, Passover, and even Christmas and Easter. After Hanukkah, the "Feast of Lights," when we lit orange candles tucked into the brass menorah in the kitchen, Daddy would go out with us on Christmas Eve to get a misshapen leftover Christmas tree. He would fix it up and deck it out with old lights from Germany, each one carefully unwrapped from a storage case, and lovingly handled. Tinsel made them sparkle and we topped the tree with a star. The money we saved for weeks before Christmas was spent on gifts at Woolworth's. Momma and Daddy had gifts for us under the tree on Christmas morning.

I still wonder at my father's independent spirit. Dad loved this country and enjoyed all of its holidays, including those that were more specifically Christian. While the Hanukkah candles burned in one room, he set up a symbol of Christ's birth in another. On Easter Sunday, Daddy would give Momma a decorated chocolate egg which we all enjoyed eating. To him, these departures from Jewish ritual were not sacreligious, but taught us respect for holidays enjoyed by some of our neighbors. With few pleasures, these events offered another chance to have a good time.

RADIO, HOLLYWOOD AND CONEY ISLAND

Everyone needed a little relief from economic disasters. Our family, like millions of others, turned to the radio to lift our spirits. With the flip of a switch we could tune in to Edgar Bergen and Charlie McCarthy on the "Chase and Sanborn Hour," or get a laugh with Jack Benny and Fred Allen.

On Halloween night, 1938, Orson Welles made history when he narrated his fantasy of the "War of the Worlds" and sent a tidal wave of terror that swept the nation, but had little effect on us.

We could even set our clocks by radio routines. If it was Monday night at 9 p.m., we gathered around for "Lux Radio Theater." On Tuesday it was "Fibber McGee and Molly," on Wednesday "One Man's Family," Thursday, "The Green Hornet" and on Friday one of my favorites, "First Nighter," when New York swells, Barbara Luddy and Les Tremayne were ushered to seats on the aisle of a theater on the Rialto. We never listened to daytime soap operas that were quite popular, since the family was always too busy.

During the stifling days of summer, without benefit of swirling fans to circulate air in the house, we sought relief at Coney Island. The beach was the seashore resort for millions of New Yorkers for a nickel a trip. Dad would wake us early, pack fried pepper, feta cheese or *kashkaval* (goat cheese) sandwiches into an old cardboard suitcase and we would be on the subway by 8 a.m. "We have to get a spot in the shade," he insisted. Dad would hammer discarded ice cream pop sticks into the struts of the pier, creating pegs for our clothes.

With no beach chairs or umbrellas, we hovered for

protection from the sun under the pier which jutted out into the ocean.

Clarie had a fair complexion and had to stay out of the sun, and Charlotte would stay with her. She burned anyway and had to be slathered with cooling Noxzema cream when everyone returned home.

Each of us had a claim on some sort of bathing suit which was generally woolly, itchy and had little to do with style, serving more as a cover-up.

Sometimes it would be a big affair with Julie and Marie's families along for the outing. Then we would race around with cousins and near cousins, sipping cool orange-ade prepared by Marie, and savoring the goodies offered from each other's picnic.

We never thought of asking for money to enjoy the many rides, souvenirs or treats sold at boardwalk stands. The knishes, soft ice cream, caramel coated apples and colorful popcorn were inviting. Everything and anything on a string was offered by hawkers to wide-eyed children, from balloons, rubber monkeys and snakes, to ballerinas and rubber fish. But we wouldn't embarrass our parents by asking for toys and goodies they couldn't afford.

On occasional strolls on the boardwalk promenade, we watched people whirl around on the carousel or slowly circle on the ferris wheel. I admired the brave who ventured the parachute jump, plunging 200 feet like falling petals to the wonder of a gawking crowd. After a while envy faded, replaced by the possibility that things would be better when we grew up.

The legacy of "doing without" that was nurtured

during the lean years was etched into our behavior and remains with all of us to this day, as we tend to justify or merit what we purchase.

By 3 p.m., sunburnt, sweaty and covered with sand, we piled into the crowded subway cars and headed home for a shower. Mom never enjoyed these trips. Most of the time she was busy serving others, staying in the shade and waiting to go back to the place she loved best: home and the company of her mother.

HOLLYWOOD

I wonder if my obsession with the movies stems from my family's needs. The movies defined our world before TV. It was a celluloid paradise often described by intellectuals as propaganda for emotional monotony, as it depicted naive morality, sham luxury, haphazard etiquette and grotesque exaggeration of the comic.

"On Saturdays, with a nickel in our pocket and a nourishing lunch packed into a paper bag, we headed for the movies," said Essie. "Sometimes I took all of the younger children and was called 'the little mother.'"

The order of elegance of movie houses in our neighborhood started with the Metro at the bargain price of three cents a ticket, up the scale to the Colony, Senate, Walker or Marboro on Bay Parkway, which was considered classy for a 25-cent admission.

The Walker, named in honor of New York's infamous mayor/playboy Jimmy Walker, was an elegant movie house with carpets, comfortable seating, chandeliers, a mezzanine, loge and balconies reached by a marble stairway. Dad took Essie to the Walker for a vaudeville show and movie.

By the 1950s, The Walker began to showcase Italian films for new area residents. Recently it was converted to a vertical shopping mall, losing a bid to remain as a historic landmark; it didn't pay!

The level of noise increased as you went down the movie palace scale. So did the crunch on the floor, the smell of wet baby diapers and the condition of the matron or usher, harried souls who spent their time chasing kids up and down the aisles, in and out of the movie house.

Nevertheless it was a convenient haven for escape. Under cover of darkness, with silence and sighs, millions were helped to survive the more dreary periods of the Depression.

Sexy Clark Gable, Mr. Christian in "Mutiny on the Bounty," was every woman's matinee idol. Whether it was lusty Jean Harlow in a slinky gown, sharp tongued Bette Davis telling off a string of husbands, Fred and Ginger singing and dancing in musical froth, or Mickey Rooney as Andy Hardy, America's typical small town boy, the big screen met the needs of a hungry audience searching for a dream.

A single movie was recycled in our home as we retold the story to our grandmother and anyone else who would listen. While I can't remember the title of a recent video rental, I could still recall the cast, characters and plot of any film I saw in the 30s and 40s, and even some of the dialogue.

Marie and Mom took turns escorting Grandma to the Metro on a Monday for the three-cent admission. The splendor of the big screen in an American movie house was a treat. Mom enjoyed the stories of triumph over hardship more than the light hearted musicals. She recalled "Symphony for Six Million," "Tobacco Road" and "The Grapes of Wrath" in infinite detail.

The lives of rags-to-riches stars, persevering young hopefuls from the wrong side of the tracks of sleepy American towns, were the kind of movie magazine stories that inspired thousands of immigrants. These starry-eyed kids were also immigrants in the foreign land of the rich and famous, and they made it!

Everybody went to the movies. Babies were nursed in the comfort of darkness, diapers were changed, sandwiches consumed and peanut shells deposited under the seats. Half the immigrant audience that piled into the Metro didn't understand English and chatted in Yiddish, Italian, Greek, Syrian, Turkish or Ladino; the other half was translating, loudly. Marie, a good cook and a hearty eater, was always well-fortified with a load of fruit and nuts to get through the day.

Amid the din of hundreds of people we managed to hear every word, usually staying after the double feature ended to see the main attraction once again. On summer days when the temperature topped 90 degrees, we headed for the air-cooled movie house and sought five hours of refuge from the heat.

Who needed schedules? On Saturdays we were first on line at noon when the doors opened, and stayed for the entire program. The Saturday marathon opened with a slew of cartoons followed by a newsreel, where we got a glimpse of what was happening coast to coast and abroad. Cliffhanger serials like Flash Gordon, preview trailers, called "coming attractions" and a B movie kept everyone pasted to their seat till the sun went down.

> **Charlotte**: To get kids and adults to fill the movie house, plaster statuettes with paint kits were distributed as promotions. Wednesdays and Thursdays were dish nights when people all over the country collected flower-trimmed earthenware. Brightly colored Fiestaware give-aways have since become quite valuable. Once, an over-run on gravy boats inspired one manager to pass them off as the week's selection for a few consecutive Thursdays. Poor misguided man; his life wasn't worth the dime for two tickets as he was pelted by the irate audience with their excess gravy boats.

In Manhattan several Times Square theaters only showed newsreels for the addicted. Some all-night movie houses catered to those who needed a place to take a nap, couples without cars who wanted to neck for a few hours, and insomniacs or cinema lovers who could never get enough movie time. On New Year's Eve the adventurous waited for the sun to rise huddled in the all-nighters, boasting to friends back in Brooklyn, "we stayed up all night."

Julie was obsessed with Hollywood. She memorized the names of stars and details of their life and loves as presented in movie magazines. She lived a fantasy life, convinced that she missed her calling as a movie star.

Essie also always wanted to be in the theater and starred in many school productions, but it was never to be. The closest she got was as an adult student studying drama at Kingsboro Community College.

The four sisters in 1945 in Brooklyn, New York. Sitting: Essie. Rear: Clarie, Charlotte, and Gloria (standing in front).

THE HOUSE ON
66TH STREET

Mi casa, mi nido.
My home, my nest.

From the outside, 1926-66th Street in Brooklyn's Bensonhurst section conformed to the 1920s semi-detached houses that sprung up in new middle class neighborhoods as the borough developed.

Only a few blocks from the Seabeach subway train (now the "N" line), the location was ideal for commuting to work, raising children, shopping enjoying the comfort of a private home, and tending a small garden.

By the early 1930s, the two small bedrooms at the rear of the house were tightly furnished with non descript depression era items. Beds were within inches of each other and no one was ever lonely at night.

When Dr. Beller, the dentist, moved out of the second floor apartment, Julie moved into the lower floor with her family and my Grandparents. Eventually, in the late 1940s, after many arguments with Julie, Grandma moved upstairs.

My grandfather Jacob died in 1941. The sweetest and gentlest of men with a warm, winning smile, he was intelligent and caring, until a stroke took his life. He often bounced us on his knee as he sang *"Samiotisa"* or *"La Farfaleta,"* an Italian nursery rhyme. *"Otra vez,"* we would shout, do it again! And, he would lift us up without complaint to repeat the game.

I often wondered how Mom perceived marriage. Her father was a patient, warmhearted gem, and her husband, basically a decent person, was often tyrannical.

My parents always occupied the master bedroom with one child or another in a nearby bed. The "small" bedroom was originally Essie's room as Charlotte and Clarie had twin beds in the "music room" adjacent to the parlor.

Through the years the small bedroom changed hands several times. Marcus Marache, a French-speaking Moroccan Jew who reminded me of Peter Lorre, rented the room for a few years. Marache, a restaurant cook, was a good friend to the family until his death in the late 1940s.

During World War II, Essie and her infant son Jerry occupied the bedroom until her husband Morris returned from the service. Their first home was in a quonset hut in the Bath Beach area near Gravesend Bay in Brooklyn that was built hurriedly to accommodate veterans during the post-war housing shortage.

I transferred from my parents' bedroom to Grandma's small room when I was about eleven. A table for essentials separated the two beds. Sharing this room with my grandmother was one of the highlights of my life. She often eased my fears, helped me through teen-age turbulence and was the voice of reason, serving as a buffer between Mom and me, as we both could be very stubborn.

Rachel Saltiel, a large featured woman, was not considered beautiful, yet she was a clear thinker, had a sense of humor and arms that enveloped us all. I liked to watch her comb out her long, gray hair, braid it and wrap it into a bun. On winter afternoons she would cut out a few *jubas de basma*, serviceable cotton dresses with a well placed collar to be worn throughout the year; she never bought a dress.

Honeysuckle climbed the brick exterior at the back of the house and wound its way into the window of our little room. Leaning on the sill I could look out to a blossoming cherry tree and the narrow garden, often commenting to Grandma on the fussiness of superneat neighbors, who busily pruned plants and swept yards.

The cracked concrete in front of the two-car garage in the back yard led to a gated garden. Dad tended a patch of mint leaves to flavor tea and an arbor of moist clusters of purple grapes which also produced wide, deep green leaves suitable for *yaprakes* stuffed with spicy rice.

Flower beds of irises and daffodils were surrounded by rambling roses. A fig tree gave the garden another touch of Mediterranean life.

"Daddy used to string up lights and set up a bridge a table and two chairs under the arbor," relates Charlotte. "On summer nights he and Marie's husband James would sit down for a quiet game of gin rummy."

It was on warm, summer days when Mom leaned out the back window to hang clothes that she would hold brief conversations with Sara Levitt or Lena Goldapple, *Ashkenazy* women pinning up their wet wash on the lines strung between houses. These neighbors were cordial and available in time of need, but never shared a cup of coffee.

The music room/bedroom had no sign of music and was separated from the parlor by a heavy drape. A pass-though window connected to a porch, icy in winter, but a cool sanctuary on hot summer nights. The many-windowed porch also offered everyone a viewing post of the passing parade of neighbors in holiday clothing, children crossing the street, fire engines screeching to a rescue, all beats in the rhythm of life on the block.

As familiar people passed, we named them after what they resembled, said or did. There was *la puntuda* or *la fithiendo*, the snobs; *la maestra*, the teacher; *la de las patas gordas*, the woman with the fat legs; *la huesuda*, the skinny, bony one; *el encamburado*, the hunchback; *la hazina la topi*, a woman always complaining of her illnesses; and *la zingana*, an over-dressed woman who looked like a gypsy. Occasionally, we would try to turn Yiddish into Ladino, when we referred to *ziggizun*, a woman who always began her conversations with *zei gesunt*, wishing us good health in Yiddish.

The kitchen, the heartbeat of our home, had a 30s deco-style metal-topped table with a silverware draw. Since someone was always cutting a slice of crusty bread and smearing it with butter or drizzling it with olive oil and a powdering of grated romano cheese, Mom was continually wiping crumbs.

When the floor got crunchy, she would pull out the broom and announce, *"tengo que dar una barrida."* I have to sweep; no one got up, instead they merely lifted their feet.

Sometimes on hot summer days when I was in the middle of a street game I would call up for something to eat. Mom would wrap up one of these unique, oily cheese sandwiches in wax paper and fling it out the window into my waiting arms.

While it was Mom who met first light each day, we were all shaken awake by 7 a.m., even on weekends! The philosophy prevailed that *quien se levanta de manana, viste en seda*, the early riser will be dressed in silk!

After breakfast dishes were cleared, two kitchen chairs which supported a flat board covered with a towel were set up to iron clothes for school or work.

The inventory for six, sometimes seven, residents was minimal in this bare bones home with few conveniences, amenities or appliances.

Our dining room featured a high, two-doored whiskey cabinet: a short, two door cabinet that held bottles of *raki* (anisette liquer), some shot glasses and a few wine bottles that always seemed to be half full. Linoleum covered the floors throughout the house and was changed when we added fresh paint to the rooms. Only the living room was covered with an oriental rug. We had heard about people who had wall-to-wall carpeting but to us it seemed impossibly extravagant and impractical; after all, you can't mop a carpet!

Above the whiskey table hung a professional photograph of me. During a Sunday stroll in Central Park in 1942, Dad was approached by a free-lance photographer for *Life Magazine* who asked to take "a picture of the little girl." I was seven years old, dressed up in a white shantung blouse and blue silk pinafore, a lovely outfit Mom bought for Essie and Morris' wedding. Several weeks after the "shoot," we received an 8x10 print in the mail, and it immediately was framed and found a place of honor in our home.

That photograph hangs in the corridor of my house in Pennsylvania and reminds me that even at that age I was looking wistfully toward finding a place in the world, a pursuit that still motivates 55 years later.

A dark, mahogany china closet with bow front window and curved legs held a few pieces of crystal, an ornate, 1920s-style coffee service encrusted with dragons, and made-in-Japan gold-rimmed flowered chinaware reserved for special occasions like Passover.

The big, dark oval table, supported by a heavy wooden base furnished our formal dining room. On special holidays Dad sat at the head of the table in the sole armchair while Mom and children occupied one of the six slat-backed chairs. This table held everything—our books, our holidays, snacks for visitors, the seder presentation and the groaning board of sweets on *noche de mimona* (end of Passover ritual).

A 1920s-style crystal chandelier hung over the table, one of the few elegant remnants of the home attesting to its former affluence. We gathered around the table during tragic events, births, deaths, marriage plans and to decorate our annual Christmas tree.

The paneled walls above the cozy loveseat held framed copies of *New York Sunday News* color photos of Franklin D. Roosevelt and the planting of the flag on Iwo Jima. Roosevelt was a strong presence in our home. Although my parents had differing political opinions, my father tolerated Mother's passion for the formidable leader. Mom never wanted to forget Iwo Jima, the event that marked the end of the conflict that devastated what was left of the family in Salonica. Without a camera we relied on Jack, Julie's husband, to take a few photos of some of the highlights in our lives.

Windows throughout the house weren't covered with heavy curtains but opened to the sun as Mom declared that *"el aire fresco haze la casa mas espaciosa*, fresh air makes the house more spacious."

When I bought a home in rural Pennsylvania, I thought of my mother and her distaste for clutter. Ours is bright, airy, full of light, and faces forests and fields. Whenever I buy a piece of furniture, I manage to throw out another to avoid excess. She would have loved it here.

We never owned a car, but the two-bay garage provided a small income of four dollars a month from a steady renter. The garage served as an ideal hideout during summer hide-and-seek marathons on the block and a get-away play area on rainy days.

The dark basement was a scary yet intriguing place for me, since it held the discards of the two families as well as the mechanics of heating and plumbing that made the house function. My father's under-the-staircase workshop held tools, lubricants, old and new nails, a vise and some of the basics for minor repairs.

Descending the stairs one could smell the fermenting mash, as Dad hand-pressed red and white grapes in a corner of one of the dingy rooms. In addition to table wine he also made *raki* (anisette) and beer. We were always amazed by his resourcefulness.

On freezing winter mornings Mom would get up before the sun rose and head down to the gloom of the basement to face the bins where she shoveled coal into the furnace, dreading the appearance of rodents or stray cats that found their way to some warmth through a broken window. Eventually, in the 1950s we converted to oil and she finally found some respite from this onerous chore.

"For a few years we had a handyman feed the fire and empty the ashes," says Clarie. "But, when Patsy quit, Mama would tend the coal stove so that we could awaken to a warm house."

Laundry, which was done on a washboard, hung on lines strung in the basement during winter months and made the dingy, damp area even more ominous. When Mom finally stopped scrubbing on the board and sent bundles out to Clime Laundry for "wet wash," they were returned clean by Mr. Heimovich ready for hanging, but we never owned a washing machine on 66th Street.

By the 1950s, Mom relied on the do-it-yourself washer/dryer stores springing up all over the neighborhood. She and Essie finally had their own washer when they bought the house on 63rd Street in the 1970s. She was 70 years old.

Old bikes, a doll carriage, three of the Dionne quintuplet dolls, a single roller skate, high black ice skates, a child's sled, a Chinese checker board and dozens of other

How did
Ash. treat Onem?

"leftovers" in the nooks and crannies of the basement evoke memories in all of us; some are painful, many pleasant.

To this day 66th Street is home and always will be. It was in the kitchen or around the dining room table, eating hot food or sweet treats, that we argued, listened and learned about women, men, raising children, getting an education and "making do."

Life on 66th Street was a mixed bag. For many reasons, the local Ashkenazim treated us as outsiders, a minority within a minority, considered neither fish nor fowl to the neighbors. Yiddish speaking neighbors distrusted Sephardics who claimed to be Jews but who appeared decidedly different. In some cases our darker complexions, the "something resembling Spanish" which we spoke, set us apart.

Aromas from our kitchen were also unlike those of other Jewish homes. We had never tasted the eastern European foods like gefilte fish, borscht, potato *kugel* (pudding) schav or stuffed derma. Our food was more highly seasoned and often drenched in tomato sauce and olive oil. Our liturgical Hebrew was accented and many of our rituals varied from what the other Jewish neighbors were accustomed to.

For centuries Ashkenazic Jews and Sephardic Jews have misunderstood each other. Wherever Sephardic Jews have been in a majority, whether in Salonica, Constantinople, Amsterdam, London, New York or Palestine, they looked down upon the Ashkenazim. When the tide turned and the Ashkenazim formed a powerful majority, they did not turn in hostility to the Sephardim but chose to show forbearance, providing assistance to downtrodden brothers.

109

Sephardim tended to isolate themselves in small communities similar to their homelands, and efforts to consolidate mutual aid societies failed. The tendency of Saloniklis to form communities around their synagogue was loosely evident in our life in Brooklyn.

During the course of many years, as we made friends in school and neighbors began to understand our work and education ethic, we partly integrated with the Ashkenazaic community. While we didn't attend each other's parties and celebrations, we maintained mutual respect.

My parents' facility with Latin-based languages allowed them to establish a relationship with the growing Italian population on the block, and good relations exist to this day.

As far as the local Sephardi, our house was "welcoming," like a European outpost! Mom believed in *as bien, no mires a quien*: do good, no matter to whom.

"People often just dropped in to rejoice or lament," adds Clarie. Someone was always home and no appointment was needed." The copper *librik*, which produced sweet, thick coffee, was ready on the stove, and a supply of *rosquitas* (doughy orange-flavored biscuits) piled on a serving dish magically appeared in the center of the table.

Some people came to repeat the story of their lives and their plight dozens of times. It didn't matter; the newer frequently increasingly dramatic version was more exciting.

REBECCA BENDINA

Rebecca, Mom's dearest friend, would arrive in the morning at about 10 a.m. With children at school and husbands

110

at work, it was just the right time after the long yawn of the morning for a snack of *boyos* (buns), cheese, olives or bread smeared with *havia* (fish roe spread).

As she climbed the long flight of stairs, Mom would say, "*Que haber Rebecca*? (what's new)?"

What an optimistic, jovial, smiling, delightful woman she was. Raised as a street waif in Istanbul, Rebecca was flush with a successful marriage to Pepo, a Moroccan who held a secure civil service job with the sanitation department. Rebecca bore eight sons whose ages matched ours. Her only daughter lived with her mother till Rebecca died.

The two friends would often hint at future marriages between Rebecca's sons and Marguerite's daughters, but it never was seriously considered. Her sons married women she liked and some who she didn't; but she always treated them with respect. Rebecca and Mom were as different as day and night, and so were their offspring.

Rebecca was chubby, loved bright floral print dresses, high heels, glittery costume jewelry, and make-up. Mom wore subdued colors, serviceable shoes and a touch of powder on special occasions. While Mom was educated and restrained, Rebecca was flamboyant, carefree and poorly educated, yet they complemented each other and remained faithful for a lifetime.

For me, the arrival of this woman was like a burst of sunshine in our kitchen. Witty, generous and accepting, she told funny stories and knew all the neighborhood gossip about *los Turkinos, los Yanotes los Monastirlis*, Sephardim from the towns and villages of Turkey and Greece.

111

Rebecca would relate her dreams, asking Mom and Grandma to interpret *los suenos*. Dreams, revealing the dark side of reason exposed in the night, had to be analyzed and understood. It was believed that voices from the past or present were helping us with hard decisions, sending warnings or allaying fears.

One morning, when I was about eight years old, I woke up crying. "I dreamt that you died," I sobbed as I held onto Mom.

"Death means life," she assured me. "I will always be here to care for you."

After Daddy died, she would claim that he visited her when she needed advice. Usually it referred to something she had intended to do anyway; she just wanted a second opinion!

In time of need Rebecca would arrive at all hours of the night, minus her make-up, but with an armful of home cooked foods. When Dad died in 1956 and funeral arrangements were being made, she came to our home at 2 a.m., took control of the household, got on hands and knees, scrubbed the floors and put everything in order before the arrival of mourners.

"When Charlotte earned a Ph.D. in chemistry from Columbia University, this uneducated woman did not try to hobnob with scholars and professors in the dining room," mentioned Clarie. "Instead she rolled up her sleeves in the kitchen, and rolled out the pizza dough for the party cele-brating my sister's success." Rebecca was fond of us and took pride in our accomplishments as though we were her own.

112

Mom was not well enough to attend Rebecca's funeral, but she penned a eulogy which Essie read at the service. "Good bye, sister of my heart," she wrote—"*Hermana de mi corazon,* I will never forget you."

Mom's sister Julie was more foe than friend, embarrassing her, spreading nasty rumors, *una pelejona* (contentious type), arguing constantly. Marguerite and Rebecca, two immigrant women from different parts of the Levant found each other in New York City and never exchanged a cross word, as they firmly anchored each other's lives.

A BEAUTIFUL FACE

I doubt if my mother looked into a mirror more than once a day as she did up her hair with a few pins. No rouge tinged her cheeks and no lipstick colored her lips. Whereas Aunt Julie pushed her vanity button wherever she went, Mom had little interest in make up, clothes or the latest fashions. Her dark brown eyes, jet black hair, broad brow and intelligent face was a template of calm and caring.

Mom wasn't a raving beauty, yet there was something warm and sensual about her. It was evident to others when shortly after the family's arrival in America, she had her choice among the swains on Park Avenue.

"Mom cut her hair for my wedding in 1941, and got her one and only permanent at that time," recalls Essie.

When Dad died from multiple myeloma in 1956, phone calls from elderly Sephardic widowers immediately rolled in. "No more men for me," she said. "I've been married once. That's enough." She had finally achieved a measure of independence.

Mom's hands, with shortened, unmanicured nails, told her story. Always immersed in water, they washed clothes or dishes, handled scorching hot plates, or gently braided a child's long hair. These hands were never feared, since she reached out to hug us, never to punish. In time of trouble the hands folded, unfolded and refolded, a warning that there was cause for concern.

Although she had little concept of fashion, hated corsets and toe crunching high heeled shoes, she really looked fine when she occasionally dressed up. Her joy was to admire us when we dressed up; *cheleste le va a Gloria* (blue was always my best color) and *Clarica con el pelo rojo, le va el verde,* Clarie with her reddish hair looked fine in green, *a Charlotica, morenica coma me, le va el rojo,* Charlotte with her dark complexion like Mom's looked good in red. Her girls were the smartest, the most beautiful, the best.

I don't remember Mom sitting down at any organized dinner. She always stood and served, preferring to eat in the kitchen with her mother rather than the dining room. Her best time was morning break when her veined hands surrounded a warmed-over cup of coffee and she chatted with Grandma, Julie or Rebecca, reading a letter aloud or translating another as she nibbled tasty leftovers.

This was the mileu in which we learned to listen. Children were included in the stories of Greece, the problems of children and husbands or the gossip of the neighborhood. This was basic training in coping, surviving and family values. The concept of the generation gap wasn't emphasized at the time as we understood where these strong women came from, and what it took for them to make it in another country.

Each morning, when she threw on a clean, cotton house dress, an apron and sturdy shoe, she was prepared to do her work. When the house was warm and ready, Mom would wake us up, remind us of the weather, put a hot breakfast on the table and send us to school with a kiss.

Unless the school was officially closed, we slogged through in any storm. "What if we are the only ones to show up?"

"If the school is open, someone has gotten there, and so will you. School comes first," she said emphatically. Mom didn't linger at the schoolhouse door to accompany us each day; that was our responsibility. She never checked homework; we knew what we had to do; there was no choice; and we never misbehaved or were insolent to teachers, but sensed that she would right any wrongs.

My mother was never more beautiful to me than in the fall of 1943, when I was in fourth grade.

When Miss Mary Murphy, a plain, spinsterish, dour, angry teacher conducted the first of her quarterly "nit checks" in our class, she lined the nine-year-olds in the sunlight of the tall schoolroom windows and probed our scalps with the point of pencil, hunting for head lice.

I suffered from recurring bouts of pneumonia. Mom who relied on old world habits, only occasionally washed my hair in cold weather for fear of chilling. Therefore, when Murphy

115

didn't find nits but did find a head full of dandruff, she declared to the class, "this girl's mother doesn't care for her; her scalp is dirty."

Insulted and humiliated I came home for lunch but had no appetite. "What's wrong," said Mom who could read my face. She slowly seethed as I related the incident, but she didn't want to upset me. "We will take care of it. Eat your lunch, go back to school. Don't say another word to anyone."

When Charlotte, who had just entered college, came home from afternoon classes, Mom called her into the kitchen, told her what happened and said, "Sit down and write a letter. I want an apology and I want it written well."

Mary Murphy's face blanched as she read the letter I delivered to her the following morning. "Come here," she called to me. "You know I never told the class that your head was dirty and that your mother doesn't take care of you. You are nothing but a dirty little liar."

"You did say it," I said.

"Perhaps sitting alone in another room will help you remember that I didn't," she continued.

"But you did," I insisted. While tears were always near the surface in the presence of authority, on this occasion my eyes were amazingly dry.

Murphy walked me into the empty classroom, sat me down in the back, turned off the lights and locked the door. It seemed like hours before she returned. I didn't budge, but rested my head on the desk.

"Well, did you change your mind?" she asked.

"No," I persisted. "That is what you said, and my mother told me to always tell the truth."

116

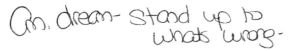
Am. dream- stand up to what's wrong-

After the bell rang, marking the end of the school day, I stayed in the yard a little longer for a few games of jump rope and "double Dutch."

Mom was sitting on the stoop waiting for me to return. "She was here. Your teacher apologized and said she was sorry she had insulted the family. No teacher would ever have excused herself in Salonica; I respect her. It's all over; forget about it."

I never forgot. What a life lesson that was for me. I have recalled that event before taking unsure steps throughout my life. My mother, an immigrant, was not afraid of teachers or retribution, but was more concerned with our self esteem, as she patiently waited for redress without storming the school. For her, this kind of action was part of the American dream; the precious right to stand up when one felt wronged, something that was never taken for granted in the land of her birth.

With the echo of my Mom's words in my ears, I have defended myself and my children when there was justification, remembering that the "lock up" in the empty classroom didn't scare me at all; I had a mother who loved me.

117

FOOD

Cuisine, like a fingerprint, defines an ethnic culture. Copeland Marks, the author of *Sephardic Cooking*, writes, "Tell me what you eat and I'll tell you where you're from." As Jewish life in Salonica overlapped Jewish life in Turkey, cuisine, especially sweets, reflected the Ottoman Empire.

Often native recipes recalled the kitchens of Spain interpreted for Ladino taste, using local products. Noting some of these recipes recalls my mother's kitchen, the hub of our home and the center of family activity.

Food was very important in our family. Mom made egg and lemon soup, chicken with prunes, *keftikas* (meatballs) and succulent beans, always served with white rice. Food was never undercooked, and everything she prepared was delicious, except for hamburgers which often emerged as overcooked patty-shaped rocks!

In the early 1960s, when my niece Michelle was enrolled in the local elementary school, she had lunch with her Grandma every day. "She always had fresh mashed potatoes and a hamburger. I used to cut up the burger, hide pieces in the potatoes, playing games with myself to find them as I ate my lunch," she remembers.

Fascinated with the nooks and crannies of the house, it was Michelle who searched through the wooden pantry on the upstairs landing which held potatoes and onions in bins, as well as a strange assortment of surplus foods the government gave to Grandma, who qualified for minimal old age assistance.

There she found tubs of peanut butter coated with oil, sugar, flour and a huge cardboard carton of Velveeta cheese. Old appliances were tucked in the lower reaches of the pantry, but hidden behind it was the coveted dessert, Sweet Nut Cake, so drenched in syrup it would last forever. "Delicious," said Michelle.

PASTEL DE MUES DULCE
(Sweet Nut Cake)

Dieters, beware! (*Sephardic Cooking* by Copeland Marks)

Cake:

> 5 eggs
>
> 1 c. sugar
>
> 1/4 c. corn or sunflower oil
>
> juice and grated rind of one orange
>
> 2 tsp. cinnamon
>
> 1 1/4 c. cake flour (or matzoh cake meal for Passover)
>
> 1 1/4 c. finely chopped, blanched almonds

Syrup:

> 2 c. sugar
>
> 2 c. water
>
> 2 tsp. lemon juice

1. Make syrup by mixing sugar and water and bringing to a boil. Add lemon juice and simmer for 10 minutes. Cool syrup.

2. Make the cake. Beat eggs until frothy, add sugar and continue beating until well mixed. Add other ingredients, one at a time, stirring into batter. Pour into an oiled and floured cake pan 13 x 9 x 2. Bake for 30 minutes at 350. Test with toothpick.

3. Pour syrup over cake and let stand for 2 hours so syrup is absorbed. Serve with a steaming cup of Turkish coffee.

Lean years or years of plenty all too frequently defined what was served in our home. Although the Depression made it difficult to provide nourishing food for a large family, Mom gave much thought to our soul as well as our bodies. Good basic meals were enhanced with herbs, spices, red wine, olive oil, and lots of TLC. Our mornings began with hot cereal or soft cooked eggs, and a spoonful of the dreaded cod liver oil to keep us healthy.

By 10 a.m. Mom, Grandma and Aunt Julie sat down *para una taza de kafe* with some *rosquitas* for dunking, or a plate of reheated delicious leftovers. Several times a week Rebecca Bendinawould arrive in time for the coffee break with some *havia* (known in Greek cuisine as Taramosalata, a fish spread made from shad roe). Like a scene out of *el cortijo*, the old courtyard in Salonica, the women set the *librik* (copper coffee pot) on the stove and huddled together, catching up on family gossip as Grandma presided over the table.

Rosquitas
(Cookies)

4 eggs	4 1/2 c. flour
1 c. sugar	4 tsp. baking powder
1/2 c. vegetable oil	

(sometimes Mom added orange juice or rind)

Beat eggs with a fork. Add sugar, beating well, then oil. Beat well.

Add flour and the baking powder a little at a time until it forms a smooth dough. Roll out, cut into 1/4-inch strips and roll these strips into 4-inch tubes. Make a circle, pinch ends together. Bake in 350-degree oven till lightly browned, about 20 minutes.

The informal morning breaks provided these women with a combination extended family and a dose of grass roots counseling. The wisdom gained over the centuries in one ancient land was translated to the values and expectations of a modern, dynamic society in the most exciting city in the world.

It was while sitting around the table (children were welcome, respected and recognized even though they were expected to mind their manners) that I learned lessons in compromise and negotiation, as well as perseverance and survival, plus a little slyness when necessary.

Sixty years later I still look forward to a monthly lunch with "the girls," my sisters. Essie, the oldest, has a wealth of recipes at her fingertips and always puts together a meal that is delightful and takes us back to our childhood.

One of my favorites is her ground meat pie. The variations on the filling for this recipe which have included spinach and cheese, eggplant or leeks are can be as exciting as the cook, and Essie always adds a seasonal touch.

SFONGATO DE CARNE
(Ground Beef Pie) Easy recipe.

1 onion chopped finely	1 tsp. salt
1 lb. ground beef	1/2 tsp. ground pepper
2 tbsp. chopped parsley	1 egg

To this can be added baked chopped eggplant, mushrooms, sauteed vegetables or little bits of tasty leftovers. In some countries it was varied with the addition of nuts and raisins for a sweeter taste.

Essie prepares the meat and spreads it out in a frozen pie crust. If she has the time, she makes one from scratch.

Bake in a 350-degree oven till a toothpick indicates that it has solidified. Cut into wedges and serve hot with a salad and crusty bread.

Here's a great salad to accompany the meat pie.

TOMAT Y PIMENTON
(Tomato and Pepper Salad)

Broil peppers to char the skin. Put them in a paper bag for about 10 minutes which will steam them and loosen the skin. Remove skin and rinse under cold water. Cut open peppers, discard seeds, stems and ribs, and cut flesh into 1/2-inch strips.

Arrange peppers with tomato wedges on a platter and drizzle with a mixture of vinegar and olive oil to taste.

We often mopped up leftover dressing with slices of crusty bread.

Nothing was wasted in our home. Pumpkin seeds were roasted into *pepitas*; stale bread became a bread pudding or croutons to accompany soup. *Pan Bollido* (boiled bread) was made by adding stale cubes to boiled water. After draining, a little oil and grated cheese made a tasty lunch. "We knew poor people in Salonica who sometimes had to resort to living on *pan y queshcos* (bread and pits or seeds)," said Mom, when she figuratively wanted to emphasize people's resourcefulness.

Each and every day something was bubbling on the stove or baking in the oven of the busy kitchen. There were dozens of variations of *sfongatos* with fillings that reflected market buys. Without a good refrigerator or large freezer,

Mom relied on available vegetables to enrich her stews, and the variations were in tune to the rhythm of the four seasons.

In spite of loving all things French, Mom was repelled by the smell of garlic and refused to cook with it. "*Ay, el ajo me da asco,*(garlic disgusts me)," she would say. She could detect the smell on those who even cooked with garlic, as it permeated their clothes. Dad had to eat food from other kitchens to enjoy the lift garlic gives to food. In later years, after reading the studies on the healthy properties of garlic, Mom admitted that it was a good bulb, but in tablet form only!

Although the 20th century intruded even in our kitchen, Mom, Julie and Grandma would often revert to the seasonal threads that ran through life in Salonica. In late autumn jam making would begin as the house became fragrant with the smell of steaming fruit boiling in large copper kettles. Preserves and jams for the year were made from quince, oranges, grapefruits, mini-eggplants, lemons and even watermelon rinds. These *dulces* and *bimbrillos* (candied fruits) were stored in the wooden cupboard off the back staircase of our home.

Bimbrilo
(Quince Sweets)

2 lbs. quinces (about 3 fruits)
2/3 c. water
pinch of salt
sugar to equal quince pulp
juice of 1 lemon

Cut up quince, discard core. Leave skin on and simmer in water and salt in covered pan for about 40 minutes.

When quince is soft, peel it, and mash it with an equal amount of sugar. Mix well, let stand in covered pan overnight.

In morning, add lemon juice and simmer while stirring until pulp forms a ball. Cool.

Roll into tablespoon-sized balls, let solidify and cool.

Grandma often helped Mom with painstaking jobs such as rolling out the dough for homemade noodles or pastries on a *tavlero* (a wide board). *Fideos*, tiny bits of egg-rich noodle dough, were used to thicken and enrich winter soups. Piecrusts, rolled paper thin were stuffed with meat for *pasteles* or *samsadas* filled with sugared nutmeats. *Yaprakes*, cold spicy rice, studded with pine nuts and wrapped in grapevine leaves were featured at every Saloniklis buffet table.

By the end of the 1940s, Mom and Grandma no longer made their own fillo dough for the finger-licking honey drenched *baklavas* prepared for Jewish holidays. Local groceries lifted that burden when they were able to package and preserve factory produced fillo.

One dreary Sunday when I was in high school, I decided to bake a cake that emerged as an inedible disaster. Mom took the cake, added some new ingredients, recycled and rebaked it. It wasn't exactly fit for a king, but amazingly, while still warm it tasted pretty good.

On winter evenings, after the main meal, Mom would present Daddy with a plate of beef bones *(huesos)* used to flavor vegetable-barley soup. Daddy would extract the marrow and clinging globs of fat, sprinkle them liberally with salt and offer a taste to his girls. As the baby of the family I had first bid on a few forkfuls of this unusual delicacy, an item I haven't seen on anyone's dinner table in 50 years! It was like mainlining undiluted cholesterol!

In the late 1930s and early 1940s Mom would occasionally stop at the Syrian grocery store on 20th Avenue in Bensonhurst. The burlap sacks of dried peas, beans and lentils, the fresh baked pita breads, the trays of assorted Greek olives, boxes of sugar-dusted *locoum* (jellied, aromatic fruit-flavored candy) and the huge cans of olive oil reminded her of the busy, noisy markets of Salonica.

Although she eventually adjusted to the more sanitized supermarkets that sprang up after the Second World War and enjoyed food shopping with Clarie, she continued to buy fresh Italian bread at the local *panaderia,* inviting us to, *senta y come, el pan esta fresco y caliente* (sit and eat, the bread is fresh and warm). She never succumbed to the freezer-microwave culture.

"On summer Sundays in the late 1930s and early 40s, we would go to Sheepshead Bay for mackerel," remembers Clarie. "When Daddy brought the fresh fish home, he often brought along some Moroccan cronies. After cleaning the fish, Mom would spend hours dipping, breading and frying for a crowd."

Joe Sananes wasn't the kind of man who ever changed a diaper or fed a baby, but he did enjoy cooking Sunday breakfast like other American husbands. Out would come the stove-top cast iron griddle as he fried up batches of made-from-scratch pancakes, eggy french toast or apple fritters.

In preparation for the holidays Dad would pull out a huge, marble slab that was tucked behind the ice box. After placing it on the kitchen table, he would roll out a honeyed, nutty, sesame paste which had been boiled in a large cauldron. When it was cooled, Dad cut diamond-shaped candies, and we would eagerly scoop up the trimmed edges. Cellophane-wrapped sesame candies sold today bear little resemblance to his traditional Moroccan goodies.

In the Moroccan Sephardic tradition, *Noche de Mimona* (the last night of Passover) was devoted to visiting. Families prepared a "sweet table," with pastries and symbols of spring and fertility.

Daddy would prepare a platter of white flour wells which held hard boiled eggs. He then made a lattice of fava beans to decorate the arrangement. The centerpiece on the table held a large, raw shad with a dollar bill in its mouth!

For guests there were always small crystal dishes filled with *bembrillos*, candied mini-eggplants, or orange, grape-fruit, watermelon and quince rinds, served with *raki* (anisette) or Turkish coffee. The liquor cabinet in the dining room held a pink glass tray with fragile handles, and whiskey was served in matching shot glasses.

As men made the rounds during this celebration, they would taste something in each home, silently measuring a woman's talent in the kitchen. Mom never cared for this showcase, and looked forward to the door closing behind the last visitor. Breathing a sigh of relief, she was glad to get back to her routine. Nevertheless, she saw these occasions as a manifestation of respect for my father, and a willingness to accommodate his traditions.

In preparation for Rosh Hashonah, Mom and Julie, with kids in tow, would head for the kosher-killed live chicken market on 17th Avenue and 65th Street. When the budget allowed, she would try to buy four chickens, to represent her four daughters. Papa Jacob was given the odious job of plucking them in the basement.

Dozens of meals were prepared from every part of the chicken. Scalded and peeled feet and giblets created a broth that was further enriched by yolks from partly formed eggs extracted from the hens. The liver was chopped up with egg and onions or served as a separate meal.

"A single chicken was roasted, stewed or made into a fricassee with onions or prunes," recalls Essie. Parts of the same bird flavored a vegetable or noodle soup and the skin of the neck was packed like a sausage with a mixture of chopped meat, raisins and seasonings."

Small bits of chicken remaining at the bottom of a pan were combined with noodles to create another meal. Spicing was never harsh or scented, like some Mediterranean food.

Large fresh cut french fries or baked orange skins stuffed with buttery mashed potatoes, and a salad of lettuce, cucumbers, tomatoes and onions in a wine vinegar and olive oil dressing completed the meal.

I still make Mom's baked salmon loaf with potatoes, eggs, bread crumbs, chopped onions, canned salmon and parsley. It was a game of stretch-the-protein into a meal. Salmon was 19 cents a can, potatoes 1 cent a pound and eggs 2 dozen for 25 cents.

Every holiday was marked by a special culinary treat. It could be sweet pie, *fijuelas* (fried strips of dough dripping with honey), *borekas de nuez y almendras* (pastries filled with nuts and almonds), a compote of prunes and apricots, or a fresh supply of *rosquitas* (cookies). For Hanukah the Sephardim fried up puffy *bunelos con miel* (donuts drenched in honey), while neighboring Ashkenazim made *latkes* (potato pancakes). The porch, a colder area, was the storage room for delicacies. I never failed to sneak in when no one was looking, to crack off a piece of crispy, honey-drenched fijuela.

FIJUELAS
(Greeks call them Avgokalamara or Diples)

5 eggs	juice of 1 lemon
2 1/2 c. semolina or farina	1 tsp. baking soda
juice of 2 oranges	1 tsp. salt
1 1/2 c. honey	1 tbsp. cinnamon
1 1/2 c. chopped nuts (optional)	

Break eggs into bowl and add farina; add orange, lemon juice and salt. Knead to form stiff dough. Dough too soft? Add a little more farina. Take a piece, roll out on floured board as for a pastry crust and cut 3" x 2" strips.

Fold two ends to form a triangle and press with fingers to stick. There are many variations as to shape. Greeks make ties, bows or triangles and fry a few at a time in hot oil until golden.

Mom used to take long strips and skillfully place one end in the oil. As it fried, she rolled it over carefully onto a fork, until the whole strip spiraled into three or four layers.

Honey is then combined with 1/2 c. of hot water. The pastry is sprinkled with chopped nuts and thinned syrup.

Bunelos or Sfenj
(Moroccan orange donuts)

(Served by the Sephardim on Hanukah instead of potato pancakes or *latkes*, it is more like a donut. Dad used to make these.)

>2 tbsp. dry yeast
>1/4 c. fresh orange juice, warmed
>4 tbsp. granulated sugar
>3 1/2 c. flour
>grated zest of one orange
>2 eggs, lightly beaten
>4 1/2 tbsp. vegetable shortening
>oil for frying
>confectioner's sugar

1. Put yeast in bowl with about 4 tbsp. of orange juice, 1 tsp. granulated sugar, and 2 tbsp. flour. Beat well and leave until frothy for about 25 minutes.

2. Mix remaining flour with orange zest, eggs, remaining sugar and 4 tbsp. oil. Add yeast mixture and mix well.

Now add just enough orange juice to make a soft dough that holds together, adding gradually and working by hand. Knead until elastic and no longer sticky, about 15 minutes.

Pour remaining 1/2 tbsp. oil into a bowl and turn dough to grease it all over.

Cover with plastic and leave in a warm place until doubled— about 1 1/2 hours.

3. Punch down the dough and roll out to 1/3 inch thick. (No need to flour surface.) Cut into 3 1/4-inch rounds. Make a hole in the center. Deep fry in batches in 2 inches of oil over medium heat. Turn once to brown all over. Drain on paper and dust with confectioner's sugar. Makes about 20 donuts.

FIJONES
(Baked Beans in Tomato Sauce)

When Mama spoke of a woman's courage, she frequently referred to her aunt, Tia Delicia, a devoted mother who scrubbed piles of clothing daily in a wash basin and cooked for a dozen people.

Beans were a major part of the family's diet, and no one prepared *los fijones* like Tia Delicia. It was said that you had to have *"dientes de oro,"* golden teeth (discriminating taste), to properly appreciate this stick-to-the-ribs dish.

1 lb. of beans (northern or pea beans. Soak overnight then drain.)

1 large onion, diced

2 tbsp. honey

1 can tomato paste

1/4 c. olive oil

1 large soup bone or a piece of shin beef

1/2 c. red wine

Fry onion in 3 tbsp. olive oil until clear. Add all other ingredients and enough water to cover and simmer slowly for 2-3 hours or more until beans split.

During the Great Depression we ate *fijones* twice a week since Mom could buy beans at three pounds for a dime. As adults, one of the best meals she could put on the table when we visited with our children on Saturday afternoons was a deep soup dish of *fijones*, with a large slice of crusty Italian semolina bread for dipping in the wine rich sauce.

HUEVOS Y PATATAS
(also known as *quahada*)

In Spain this popular dish is called Tortilla Espanola, but various versions of this favorite all-in-one meal traveled throughout the Ottoman Empire where it was modified with local herbs and spices.

Making the *"quahada"* was my father's job on a Sunday evening. He used to compete with my Uncle Jack, another *marroquino*, as to the height and heft of the omelet.

The basic recipe requires:

> 4 large potatoes, diced
> 4-6 eggs, beaten (some of the eggs can be
> modified with egg white substitutions.
> I use 3 eggs and 3 whites. "Egg Beaters"
> doesn't work well.)
> 1 large onion, diced
> olive oil for frying

Use a teflon pan for this recipe and less oil will be needed. It also will be easier to handle.

Fry potatoes and onions until soft.

Remove, drain, cool and add the mixture to beaten eggs. Salt and pepper to taste.

Fry mixture slowly in a 1/4" of olive oil. Poke holes in it periodically to allow steam to escape as the omelet dries.

When a crust begins to form, remove from stove. Turn it over onto a large dish and then slide it back into the pan to brown the second side. Once again, poke holes to allow steam to escape.

Brown slowly. Then slide it onto a serving platter.

The key to this recipe is patience (allow two hours) and a good omelet will be crusty on the outside and dry on the inside.

Allow to cool and cut into serving wedges. An accompanying salad makes an ideal lunch.

In Spain, the Tortilla Espanola is as much a part of picnics and parties as American cold cuts. Even unheated it makes a terrific lunch.

Serves 4-6.

"If we didn't eat enough at the Passover seder, Mama would beat up an egg and lemon and add it to chicken soup to make it more tempting," mentions Charlotte. "For many years when we had an ice box, the kitchen window also served as cold storage for homemade pickles and sauerkraut stored in earthenware pots with loose tops. English sparrows nested in the oven vent near by. Since the vent was useless to us, the space was later covered with a plaster plaque of fake fruit, a popular item in the 1940s.

Mama was a good cook. Even when there wasn't enough for her, she was pushing food at us. During hot summer months she would prepare sour cream with boiled potatoes or bananas, salmon salad with chopped onions, or colored Jello layers.

One evening recently, as we sat in Essie's kitchen, recalling Mom's kitchen, all four of us came up with the same story. Friday afternoon!

On Friday afternoons, approaching 66th Street on my way home from school, I could smell the baked sheet cake and visualize the creamy topping of fresh chocolate pudding made from corn starch, cocoa and milk. "She's made it especially for me," I thought.

Clarie, who was treated to the more expensive mini-lamb chops in the hope that it would improve her appetite, thought she was making it for her. Charlotte and Essie also thought it was baked in their honor. The truth was that she baked it for each of us, and for all of us, as a treat to mark the end of another school week and the start of the weekend.

> **Clarie**: Milk was an obsession for Mom. We had to drink a quart a day. Arriving in Ellis Island she sensed that it was truly the land of milk and honey. Milk was clean, fresh, tasty, plentiful and cheap. A warm glass of milk prepared us for a restful sleep each night (she hadn't heard of the soporific qualities; it was instinctive).
>
> Wherever we went, at whatever age, the warm cupfull was waiting when we got home. Even when I dated Gino, she would put out an extra glass for him.

Why were we all so thin when so much good food and love was available? Maybe it was genetic. Mom would stand near us as we picked at our food and complain, *"mira, esta comiendo como la mosca en la olla* (look, she is eating like the fly tasting a stew)." Unfortunately, conditions change and we are now part of the millions of women who can never be too thin. As we get older and gravity pulls us toward the earth, we step off the scale determined to turn back the clock a bit by rejecting the next piece of baklava!

Our homes continue to reflect Mom's warmth and acceptance. The coffee pot perks, and cookies are always on hand to welcome visitors. We rarely worry about whose turn it is to gather the family around the dining room table. While we enjoy each other's hospitality, it is the conversation generated and the fellowship enjoyed that remains the best and most important part of the meal.

WHO'S NEXT?

Mom was obsessed with health and the survival of her four daughters. When we were sick, we didn't malinger or she wouldn't get any rest.

In the 1930s, the U.S. hadn't entered the golden age of a pill for every ill or antibiotics as a panacea to prolong life. They were the days of argyrol, iodine, mercurochrome, nose drops, spoonsful of cod liver oil, flavored rock candy, chamomile tea, and eucalyptus pouches strung around our necks in summer to ward off polio. Dozens of useless preventatives or cures were merely palliative.

Mom was firm in her belief that avoiding drafts, staying out of the rain, dry feet and less frequent baths in winter's chill were rules to live by, as the body had to be protected. When it was cold at night and the stove had been banked, hot water bottles kept our body-place warm.

Essie contracted scarlet fever, Clarie was tormented by allergies and sensitive skin plagued with severe eczema, Charlotte was hospitalized for over a month in isolation with diphtheria, I stuttered, had speech defects and suffered bouts of pneumonia from infancy until I was treated with sulfur after World War II.

Who's next? In two adjacent households of four daughters and two nieces, another sick child to pull through a crisis was always on Mom's mind. What if one of her four daughters died, could she survive?

Dr. Wilensky or Dr. Scovner paid house calls, left prescriptions and often wondered about these unusual Jews and their habits. While my parents honored the prescriptions and gave us the proper doses, they also added their own methods of healing. Along with their satchels from Salonica they carried a bag of unrecorded tricks passed down through time, in the hope of keeping children alive. Grandma relied on *sal inglesa* (Epson salts) for whatever ailed her, and although she mentioned *kenino* (quinine), the treatment for malaria in Salonica, we never needed it.

For me, the most dreaded cure-all was the "mustard plasters." After Mom determined that the only solution to the heaving cough was penetrating heat, she would begin to fry the mustard, as I steeled myself in anticipation of the poultice. Securing the steaming mush between two pieces of cloth, she applied it to the afflicted heaving chest, the hotter the better but not quite hot enough to scar for life!

A towel was immediately slapped on top of this muddy fire and the patient left to suffer till the plaster cooled and hopefully some of the phlegm dissolved. After removing the poultice, another towel was placed over the steaming chest to capture the last few rays of penetrating heat.

The heady fumes were supposed to wage war with the suffocating mucus that threatened to close down my lungs. Maybe it was fear of the mustard plasters that sent a message to the suffering brain, "Get better fast or else another will be frying up on the range!"

One of the things women from all walks of life had in common at that time were endless conversations, describing in minute detail, how their offspring were saved from the jaws of death. The grim reaper had to be outwitted as children were plagued by yearly outbreaks of polio, diphtheria, meningitis, TB, whooping cough, measles, convulsive high fevers and a textbook of ills without effective medications.

When Charlotte had diphtheria at the age of three, she was treated for over a month in an isolation ward at Kingston Avenue Hospital in Brooklyn. When she returned home, it appeared that she had lost her speech.

"She didn't speak until she finally talked to Clarie," said Mom. "She was just mad at us, but I wasn't worried. I knew *"que manana le pasara* (she would forget tomorrow)."

Imagine placing a child today in an isolation ward. Parental guilt and blaming would run rampant; the child would be damaged for life with eventual flashbacks to the horror of "the ward."

To my parents, it was a Godsend that there were doctors, nurses and clean places to treat children who would have died in the ghettos of the Mediterranean cities of their youth, and their optimism was passed along as part of the healing process.

With no antibiotics to fight off pneumonia, Mom did what she could and her TLC involved long nights of walking with a crying infant, alcohol rubs, herbal teas, aspirin, infinite patience, and sometimes a whispered prayer.

During a severe life threatening bout of pneumonia, my parents renamed me "Delicia" in the hope that a new name would sustain life. After the crisis I went back to being

139

Gloria, but on occasion she would lovingly call me Delicia.

Only the summers offered a measure of relief, but the specter of another siege of illnesses before the first month of school had ended was a virtual certainty. We all have stories to tell.

> **Essie**: One day I came home from school with an unusual blush and the new young doctor on the street, Nathan Wilensky, diagnosed scarlet fever.

> **Clarie**: When I was an infant I had convulsions as a result of high fever and was taken to Kings County Hospital. I think Daddy was in denial whenever we got sick and left the worrying to Mama.

> **Charlotte**: I was fairly healthy except for a bad case of measles and the bout with diphtheria that rotted my temporary teeth. When Clarie had pneumonia in the days before sulfa treatment, the only cure was bed rest and small amounts of brandy. Momma was a tireless nurse. When Gloria got pneumonia and was hospitalized, she returned sobbing, clutching the empty blanket.

Momma would sequester us in the small back bedroom, the same one that was later used for our boarder, Marcus Marache, a bridal suite for Essie and Morris, and eventually for Grandma when she came to live with us.

As the communicable diseases threaded their way through the family, our mother didn't panic at the responsibility, only the looming dread of losing one of us.

Throughout the winter, one of the children was always propped up in bed missing a day of school. Since both families often functioned as one, we not only caught everything from each other but from Julie's girls, Marilyn and Ray, as well.

mother-ultimate nurse
& care taker

Perpetually thin, with a lingering pallor, several of us were also poor eaters. Clarie and Charlotte were so thin that the school even considered the "Open Air Class," a placement usually reserved for children recovering from tuberculosis who required afternoon rest periods.

In the late 1940s we all endured a serious stomach virus that affected the six children in both households. Severe bouts of diarrhea, *echando la fiel* (continuous vomiting) and depression left us crying constantly. No one's pain was minimized as Mom and Julie boiled barley water into a thin soup and made chocolate pudding with water. When they were busy, Grandma, with some crochet project in hand took their place at our bedside, keeping the vigil till we were better.

In 1984, my son Bob suffered weeks of colitis that didn't respond to modern medications. In frustration I tossed the prescriptions aside, boiled up a pot of barley and gave him a few glasses of the gray, salty, tasteless broth. For dessert he was treated to a few bowls of chocolate pudding made with water. Within two days he was well and returned to college.

In retrospect, I realize that Mom was able to cope because of her strong will and her mother's help. Time, often the best of healers, worked in their favor. Grandma lightened some of Mom's burden and we weren't rushed to health before some measure of nature went to work.

As a working parent I now realize the tension that prevailed in my household when my kids got sick and I had to get on with my professional life. They must have received the unspoken message that Mom had important things to do. We were our mother's work, and her unspoken message was "Take your time, just get well."

Clarie: I was very skinny and pale and in addition to being a poor eater, I suffered from severe eczema. On Saturday mornings Mama dragged me from one clinic to another trying to find a cure to alleviate the constant itching. The doctors never imagined that it could be a food allergy, yet I've been a victim of allergies all my life. I think the cod liver oil everyone took to nourish children exacerbated the condition.

The search to ease Clarie's misery persisted until she was about 12 years old. "While Mama was watching over us in a local playground, a woman sitting on a bench nearby asked why she seemed so depressed," recalls Clarie.

"It's her incurable skin condition," she answered, "look at her, the itching is terrible. It's breaking my heart."

"If I gave you some advice would you be offended?" said the stranger.

"I'm ready to listen to any suggestion to help my daughter. We don't know what else to do; she has been to all the clinics," she explained.

"Try giving her spoonfuls of honey and fresh grapefruits daily."

How could honey and fresh fruit be harmful? It was the kind of cure Tia Delicia would have used with her children in Salonica.

Dad immediately bought jars of honey, dozens of grapefruits were sliced and served in every shape and form, hoping the nightmare would end for their little girl.

Within a few weeks Clarie's skin cleared up. "I never saw those ugly sores again," she said. "Mama felt that the woman, who was a Christian Scientist, was God sent. In retrospect, there were several factors that could have led to the improvement. I stopped taking cod liver oil, I could have had a Vitamin C deficiency, or as Mama believed, it was a miracle."

While she was busy taking care of us, Mama neglected her own health. By the time she was 40 and had endured multiple miscarriages, her hair was thin and graying, her teeth rotting from pyorrhea, and after years of shoveling coal for the furnace she needed a truss to support a hernia. Frail and worn, she was misdiagnosed as having contracted tuberculosis and didn't fear for her own life, but feared leaving her children without a mother.

When the Margaret Sanger Clinic opened in 1939 on 14th Street in Manhattan, Mom was among the first to seek contraception. She joined those who took the initiative in preventing unwanted pregnancies that threatened the lives of women and clouded their horizon.

Not for her daughters! Life would be better. No more anxiety during sexual relations and the anxious wait each month for her period. Her daughters' minds and bodies would no longer be controlled by men. Now it would be different, thank God.

GIVING ADVICE

From *los cortijos* of Salonica to the tenements of Park Avenue and the tree-lined streets of south Brooklyn, my grandmother, Rachel Benrube, brought compassion, understanding and wisdom to men, women and children in stress.

When Kate and Meyer Abulafia were in the midst of a fight, they would leave their home anytime of the day or night and come to Tia Rahel. Grandma would look at the warring couple. "You sit here," she would tell Kate, who always arrived with a handbag packed with handkerchiefs to mop up the tears. "And you, Meyer, over there." The scene was set, the couple were separated and she placed her cane as a calculated barrier between them.

"Now stop screaming and crying and tell me what happened." Before the husband and wife could begin she would turn to my mother. "Marguerite, *pone el librik y trae unas roscas.*"

Mom would bring in a tray of cookies and steaming cups of thick, sweet Turkish coffee as the story would unfold. Everyone was familiar with the rules; keep quiet while the other spoke; no clock was ticking; and the situation would be resolved or they wouldn't leave the room.

To Rachel the children came first. Adults had to learn to control their behavior. Divorce was never mentioned, although it was threatened constantly. *"No se decha a un marido para arrastar.* (You don't leave a husband to wind up as a beggars.)," she warned Kate. With no skills and no foreseeable future, what could she give her children without a father? She would warn Meyer, a cigar-smoking, jovial but stubborn Moroccan, of the result of losing his family because of indiscretions.

After tears were wiped away, coffee cups drained and the cookie crumbs collected, there would be a few jokes, some gossip, and finally kisses of farewell. Sometimes Grandma would ask my father to escort the couple home to make sure they settled in peacefully for the night.

No one could raise their voice to Grandma. She would lift her nubby cane and threaten to teach them a lesson right there and then. Huge men that would daunt most people, begged her forgiveness and promised to behave better toward their wives. It was understood that older people were wiser, and Rachel Saltiel was renowned for her good, sensible, practical advice.

Having a good name and preserving the family was paramount. *Un nombre bueno* was like money in the bank. *El nombre malo* (bad name) was like a tainted gene that could emerge in succeeding generations and in the minds of people, especially when marriage was in the works.

The idea of making an appointment and paying a stranger, although a professional, to hear about family troubles while a clock was ticking toward the 50-minute hour was unthinkable. To the immigrant Sephardi, the pros didn't know their culture or their language or how to heal their wounds. And, what was to happen the next time and the next? Because, they always knew there would be some family problem. That's married life; *esto como es el casamiento.*

I clearly remember Moshe, Grandma's distant cousin. All alone in the city, the tall funny-looking, beady-eyed man lived in a boarding house with few social contacts. Moshe had married Amelia, a lively fragile woman who had difficulty dealing with the demands of a superneat husband who was an unrelenting nagger.

"Es el que la quito loca," it was he who drove her crazy and she was put in an institution for several years," said Grandma. Moshe's only son Ralphie went from pillar to post, but was raised by his mother when she was well. The pitiful Amelia ultimately had to take her husband to court for non-payment of child support.

"Lo mandaron a la carcel por seis meses donde hacia escobas (he was jailed for six months and made brooms)," said Mom. Ralphie eventually became a professional photographer and maintained an occasional relationship with his father.

We knew that when Moshe made his biannual pilgrimage to our house, only people who shared a common history could listen to his repetitive story and the anguish of his life. Nevertheless, Mom and Grandma knew he had to talk to someone and that he had suffered for his sins.

Wise counselors today rely on family networks, significant others, knowledgeable advocates, and cultural understanding in treating their clients. In spite of some serious issues, children were rarely asked to leave the room during these episodes unless the elders felt it could be harmful for them. Without insistence we instinctively held confidentiality.

Those who didn't have a Tia Rahel in their family often found their way to our home and a sanctuary in her wisdom.

As I look back on our family dynamics I realize that we all developed a buffer in the family; one who could speak for us when we couldn't do it for ourselves. I shared a bedroom with Grandma from the time I was 10 till I was a 16 year old teenager, and count those years as a learning period on the essence of human nature. She counseled me during late night hours before we both fell asleep and during the sunny afternoons when I just hung around her room.

Grandma spoke on my behalf when I was troubled; the world always looked a little brighter after she heard my problems. Many years later as I trained as school counselor I mentioned Grandma to my professors who agreed with my point of view in modeling much of my approach on her good sense.

As I sat in my office in a typical run-down school in one of New York City's largest Latino ghettos, some of my advice to people of all persuasions was; look into your culture, find what works, seek out a significant other and always remember, the children are most important. I insisted that adults who promised to love one another should take another look at what they are doing, and to explore every possibility before they headed for splitsville.

"In addition to the Sephardic women who rang our bell at every hour of the day and night, crying and threatening to leave home, there were others," said Clarie. "After Grandma died, neighbors and friends would stream in to see Mama. The more wretched a person, the more miserable a life, the more welcome they were to spill their feelings in the warm shelter of the family kitchen."

The list was endless. Tina, a young mother of seven who lived nearby, faced problems with her unemployed husband and retarded daughter. Her mother Josie was blind, her father didn't understand the nightmare she faced, her brothers were aloof. Burdened by bills, babies and problems, all that was left of the once beautiful girl who raised the heartbeat of the boys on the block was her captivating smile. Where to turn?

One afternoon she showed up on our doorstep, one baby cradled in arms, another tugging at the hem of her dress. "Can I speak with Mrs. Sananes?" she said. Rail thin, shaking like a leaf and smoking like a chimney, she sat down near Mama who held her close for a few moments and let her cry till speech could come.

After several cups of coffee, more sobs and more tears, Mom listened to her story.

Over several cups of coffee and through more sobs and tears, Tina told her story and listened to Mama's soothing voice, hearing about others who survived. "Archie is a wonderful husband, and cares for you and the children, you are blessed," she said. "But there have to be some changes in your life and only you can make them." Although she did suggest birth control, Mom never urged Tina to violate her beliefs, but to work within them if that was the only option. Tina knew that the door to Mrs. Sananes's home was always open; she just had to ring the bell. Tina and Archie went on to have a total of nine children, and a successful business. With heavy hearts they placed their daughter in a group home and the family went on to survive and prosper.

One family, unique to the neighborhood eventually changed my perspective on where I belonged in the world. When the Andersons became our neighbors in the early 1940s, it was a culture shock for them and for us.

THE ANDERSONS

There were few cars on 66th Street in 1943. Kids ran around them, climbed behind them and hid from each other. Most people drove slowly and only on Sundays. "Watch the machine," was the call from the *va vas* (old ladies) stationed on the stoops in front of their homes.

There weren't too many changes on the block, since Brooklyn was the world and the block was "our town." But, when the van pulled up at the empty house down the street, I sensed that something was definitely different.

"New people," said Benny Todaro, who watched them park. "I hope they have kids." Few people ever "moved in." Everyone was where they wanted to be, no "ins," no "outs," no moving up. The only talk heard daily was about the war and which of the local boys were called up.

"Look at the license plate," said Joey Greenberg, who joined the committee of kids that seemed to materialize within the hour. "It's different. What's N.D.?" It couldn't be; a stranger, a family from North Dakota? As we examined a map of the U.S. in an old encyclopedia, we concluded that it might as well have been Eskimos from the North Pole. Where were the cities, the large towns? Why would anyone live so far away from the beach?

Mom peeked out of the porch window as she sized up John and Susan Anderson. "Farmers," Mom called back to my grandmother. "Who else would live up there where it's freezing all the time. They give away land in those places, they must be wheat farmers. What are they doing here?"

On a street full of greenhorns accustomed to the mysteries of the old country, changes were pregnant with great meaning, breathing life into established routines. Scared and excited, I decided to pursue the adventure. "Don't get into trouble, Gloria, *hablas mucho*, you talk too much, " said Aunt Julie, "and don't tell them much about us. It's none of their business!" For Julie, the local busybody, the new family was grist for her gossip mill.

Was that huge woman with long legs and short hair the mother? "*Mira las pachas*, look at her legs,"said Mom. "The tall 'skinny balink' must be the father." Two pairs of eyes peered through the front porch window. "It's the kids," I thought. Just like the books in school; only two, a boy and a girl.

"Luann, come on out, nothing to be afraid of," said the big mom. Luann? Among the Saras, Mollys and Josephs, this was something new.

"There's a nice little neighbor's child out here waiting to meet you." I always thought I was just the kid across the street!

As Luann emerged from the porch, I saw the blue-eyed, blonde pig-tailed image of the American child. Green with envy I watched the heroine of children's books, followed by barking Spot and cuddly Muff trot down the stairs. Here were Dick and Jane, Nancy Drew and the Bobsey Twins all rolled into one. And to complete the picture, John-John, the annoying, but lovable little brother of fiction, followed in his sister's footsteps.

Susan, their Mom who was almost six feet tall, strode down the street in black shorts and sneakers. Big John, a few inches taller, also in shorts, smoking a pipe, held his wife's hand as they examined their new neighborhood.

The block, largely populated with first generation Jewish and Italian families was stunned by the sight of two very tall people in shorts holding hands. It was like meeting aliens.

"I heard from Anna Melnick that the father was offered a job in New York and is working for a bank," said Aunt Julie.

"No banks in North Dakota?" answered my mother as she added just a little red wine to the beans for dinner. The fertile imaginations ran rampant, as each new thought began with *seria que*, it must be that....

Why would people from farms come to Brooklyn, the first stop for people from the other side. Would they make fun of us? Were our eyes too dark, our hair too thick, our noses too long, our accents too strong?

"Why didn't they just stay where they came from and leave us alone?" I asked.

"Never say such a thing Gloria," admonished Mom. "People told us to go back to where we came from not long after we landed at Ellis Island. It must have taken that woman a lot of courage to leave her home and family to come to a busy city like New York. Now like us, they are greenhorns here."

Just how much courage, we never really came to know. But we did know that the Andersons tried to make the best of their predicament. For several weeks, the family scurried about, getting settled before summer ended and the children were packed off to a big city public school.

Before long, Luann became my best friend and their son, young John Jr. just hung around with us. We spent more and more time together, talking, laughing, playing hide and seek and reading comics. One hot afternoon, Susan Anderson invited me to a peanut butter and jelly sandwich lunch in their home.

Another world opened up to me as soon as I entered their kitchen. The family sat around together and said grace before eating. Mr. Anderson helped his wife while complementing her on a delicious meal. The children asked to be excused when they finished lunch, and no one was told they had to eat each crumb, or else.

When the table was cleared, Luann sat at the piano and played one of the etudes she had been practicing, and John Jr. went into the yard to swing on the playset. Mrs. Anderson then took out the ingredients to bake cookies. Did I land in middle American heaven or WHAT!! "Nobody will believe me when I tell them about this family," I thought. *Es una mentira* (it's a lie)."

When the family planned a shore picnic on a warm Sunday and asked me to join them, I felt an instant chill. "I can't go, " I said. "My family doesn't let me go anywhere without them, I can't even sleep over at a friend's house. I can only leave my home at night when I get married!"

"Let me talk with your Mom," said Susan. I hoped she would soon forget about it; this woman just didn't understand who we were and how we lived. I didn't want to create problems and lose a nice friend.

As the first one to hear the doorbell ring, I hurriedly looked out the window to see who it was. "It's the farmer lady," I whispered to my mother, "should I tell her you're not home?"

My mother was always at home; all mothers stayed home, except when they went to the grocery. "What does she want," Mom wondered, "but since she came like a lady, invite her in."

"I just baked a batch of chocolate chip cookies," said Luann's Mom," and I thought you would like some. I'm Susan Anderson and we wanted to meet Gloria's family. She was the first one to greet us when we moved in a few months ago."

Mom wiped her hands on the stained apron, pushed back a wisp of hair and extended her hand. "Hello Susan, I'm Marguerite. Thank you for the cookies, I'll give back the dish right away," she said hurriedly. "Sit down and relax, do you want a cup of coffee? "

"She is some woman," related Mom to Aunt Julie and Grandma, as soon as the door slammed shut. "She has gone through more hardships than we can ever know." Going through hard times, *lo que sufrio la povre* (oh, what she suffered) was the ticket to my mother's heart.

"They lost their farm during the Depression and the husband, John, had to get a job at a very low salary. Now he

154

found a job in New York with the help of an old friend, and Susan is starting a new life."

"By the way, I'm letting Gloria go with them on a family picnic to Gravesend Bay," she said as an aside. "They are good people and promised me they would bring her home before dark. I just won't tell Joe."

"*Estas loca*," said Julie. "I don't trust her; she's not like us!"

When the children returned to school, Susan would drop by more often, with baked fruit breads and puddings, often holding Mom's hands as tears of homesickness were shed.

Of course, Mom told her about the fire in Salonica, the crossing from Greece, the long journey, new language, confusion and crises. She told her about life in Harlem, her first job, the matchmaker and life with father, a good man but a far cry from the American ideal.

"I'm so ashamed of crying like this, Marguerite," said Susan. "I always want to be strong. Where I come from, tears are a sign of weakness."

"It's not a sign of weakness," she answered. "You're strong, but you're also human. Remember, you are always welcome in my home, no invitations necessary. Come over and talk whenever you like. If you keep it all in, you will get nervous! The pain inside will grow and eat at you like *el gusano* (the worm)! Fortunately, I have my mother living here and we talk about everything; you don't have anyone."

The Andersons tried to maintain some semblance of their former lifestyle. They dressed for church on Sunday, Luanne and John-John went to Bible classes and Susan carried covered dishes for church picnics at the small Methodist church near 18th Avenue.

As I watched Luanne's dad kiss his wife and the children when he returned from work in the evening, it seemed like a movie of apple pie America. Amazing. The mother didn't keep secrets from her husband, the children weren't afraid of their father and everyone seemed to like each other.

Susan and John took me off the block and on to other blocks and neighborhoods, as they became immersed in the ethnic enclaves carved out by the immigrants that flooded into New York. Hand in hand, the tall, gangly couple led us through Little Italy, Little Sweden, Chinatown, down the Lower East Side and up Fifth Avenue. Back home on 66th Street, their kitchen smelled of fresh bread and hot soups, their decor comfortable and cozy.

Susan canned seasonal fruit and vegetables; the children always helped out, and lending my hand to the task gave me a chance to live their experience as they brought the heartland to "our town."

"We're going home, Marguerite," Susan said excitedly one morning in early October, 1946. "I'm going to be with my family once again, but I will miss you all so much. Although we were homesick, John and I as well as the children have enjoyed a special experience here. Sitting in your kitchen, tasting your foods and even listening to your gentle language has enriched my life."

"Make my *fijones* for your family in North Dakota," said Mom. "It's a good hearty meal, especially for farmers on a cold day. It will also remind you of our friendship."

−new friends.
from diff places

As she hugged Susan, Mom, always the writer Mom said, "We can send letters to each other. You are kind and caring people. My Gloria has learned so much these last few years; it's been good for her."

I hid under my bed while the moving van was loaded, taking the Andersons back to the mid-west; I couldn't let them see me cry, I already had a reputation for being *una llorona*, a cry baby. Within a few weeks another family moved into the detached one-family. They came from the lower east side and had a boy my age, Richie. I was twelve and old world tradition dictated that it was okay to start thinking of boys; they weren't so bad after all.

But, I missed Luann, John-John, Susan, big John and their way of life. I learned to love the smell of their home as I loved my own. Susan was my Mom when we explored New York. In her kitchen I discovered middle America. Marguerite Saltiel Sananes' kitchen introduced Luanne to the tastes and moods of Salonica. I realized that family had many different meanings and that a special friendship can be eternal. The old thicket of ignorance that separates strangers was coming down, as my world grew bigger and better.

After the odyssey with the Andersons, it took me forty years to make the decision to move to the heartland I dreamed about. Today my kitchen in Pennsylvania smells of fresh baked bread and apple pie, as well as *fijones*. I look out over farm-land, renewed and refreshed, recalling my childhood in Brooklyn and a family whose friendship helped shape my life.

THE 40s AND BEYOND

Essie was the first of six girls in the two households to get married. Lizzy Arama, a family friend, introduced the 18-year-old high school graduate to Morris Kubie, a dashing and handsome Israeli (Palestine before 1948) who was 12 years her senior.

With a jaunty panama hat perched on his head, a ready smile and winning ways, he seemed like the right husband for Marguerite's daughter, especially since he had a job as a furrier and appeared to be able to support a family. He also had a car!

On their first date, Essie was treated to a banana split, a delicacy we never experienced. On her return she described it in detail: the slices of banana base piled with many-flavored balls of ice cream, swirls of whipped cream, layers of hot fudge and coating of walnuts, to the crowning moist maraschino cherry. We drooled.

The new fiancé took us for rides around the block in his 1936 Oldsmobile, and his six brothers and their families seemed to get along nicely with ours.

1941. Although there were rumblings of war on the horizon, it appeared to be far away. Life was good, the family was emerging from the Depression and we were going to celebrate our first wedding since arriving on 66th Street.

While people lined up at the movies to see "Gone With The Wind," war was raging oceans away and debates raged regarding America's role.

With the invasion of Pearl Harbor on December 7, 1941, any hope for peace was smashed and there was no longer a question of involvement. The nation mobilized. Shortly after their honeymoon in Lakewood, New Jersey, Morris was drafted and Essie returned home, pregnant with twins.

In the same way that John Kennedy's death marked time for the next generation two decades after the surprise attack on Pearl Harbor, people would recall where they were and the response to the shock. I was seven years old when the news came over the radio. The house came alive, as Mom called Julie, she called Jack, children were roused from their beds, and everyone gathered in the living room. As I looked out of the porch window I saw lights coming on in the houses down the street; this was something that touched everyone.

Nightly radio news focused our evenings, as we followed battle maps and watched legions of young men disappear from our neighborhood, later returning to the block, showing off their impressive uniforms. Overnight, boys became men, as we relied on them to defend our country. Families who sent their children to war displayed a flag in the window; the number of stars announced how many had been drafted.

We now lived in a narrower world of women, children, older men and those unable to serve, the 4-F category. While some soldiers were decorating lockers with glossies of pin-up girls like Rita Hayworth and Betty Grable, others were facing bullets, too often returning home, crippled or maimed, with purple heart medals for courage. Their families now displayed a newer flag of sacrifice, as the name "Gold Star" mother meant death on the war front.

The world was in flames as air, land and sea battles were fought on numerous fronts. It was the first time we heard about "shell shock," which left no visible scars.

Rumblings of the plight of Jews in Poland, Czechoslovakia, Germany and throughout the rest of Europe depressed Mom and Grandma. What about Tia Bonna, Avram and their children? As correspondence faded, Mom wondered, would the Greek government protect its Jews?

Routines proceeded as always on 66th Street. Morris' fluency in Italian qualified for a stateside post in San Bernadino, California, where he supervised Italian prisoners of war. Love letters from the new groom came daily and we all took a peek inside the envelopes at messages which usually began, "My dearest sweethearts, Ethel and Jerry."

Jerry was born in August, 1941; his twin was stillborn. A frail child, he was largely raised by Mama when Essie went to work for Lerner's Shops as a bookeeper. The young 19-year-old mother and her baby now took their turn occupying the small bedroom in our house.

It wasn't easy for Mom to raise a rambunctious little boy while she tried to make life comfortable for an aging husband, but she did it. As an infant Jerry came down with whooping cough and required round the clock care to survive. After he recovered, I came down with the same illness, lost a month of school and added a few more gray hairs to my mothers head. She never complained.

On the home front women pitched in at factories and filled the jobs of the boys who went off to war. The community came together with air raid drills, bond drives, collections of paper, cooking fat, rubber and scrap metal to transform into fighting weapons.

In second grade I was given a plastic ID necklace to wear at all times in case children had to be evacuated from the city. Where would we go? Would we be taken away from our parents and sent to the Catskill Mountains? Everyone, at some level, feared for the future, or in a child's mind envisioned dramatic possibilities.

Victory gardens sprang up on small patches of soil. The summer I was nine, I proudly brought home a sizable crop of vegetables from PS. 205's summer school's garden. I was doing my part; we all were.

The school was organized into a mini-army, with student soldiers gaining rank by bringing in piles of newspaper to support the war effort.

Our fighting song was:

> Hail to the Junior Commandoes;
> We're children of 205.
> We're fighting along with our soliders
> To keep Victory's flame alive.
> So, hail to the Junior Commandoes;
> We're doing our bit at home
> To help the boys in Tokyo, Berlin and Rome.

Clarie and Charlotte were now emerging as teenagers, talking about cute sailors and soldiers, but it was all talk. By 1943, Clarie and Essie were riding the subways to work, and Charlotte, the family scholar, had entered college. There was never any question in anyone's mind that Charlotte would succeed. In addition to skipping several grades in elementary

162

Charlotte and Joe Russell in 1951. Charlotte was the first to graduate from college, later receiving a Ph.D. in chemistry.

school and junior high, she went on to stun teachers in New Utrecht High School with her brilliance.

After Charlotte walked away with virtually every prize, medal and monetary award at her high school graduation in 1948 where she was the valedictorian, the school went one step further and painted her name in gold on a special roll of honor in the lobby. Charlotte Sananes was the talk of the neighborhood and has been one of the sources of family pride.

Sometimes Mom would pull her daughter's medals out of a red velvet sack and show them to me. While we all were high achievers, Charlotte was someone we always admired and respected. Sibling rivalry in this area of scholarship wasn't even considered. She was then and continues to be one of the jewels of our family's generation.

By the time she was 24 years old, Charlotte earned a Ph.D. in chemistry from Columbia University and entered the halls of academe. She has been a professor at City University for the past 45 years where she has impacted on the lives of hundreds of students, many like herself, the first in their family to honor their immigrant parents.

While they sang the latest songs, practiced the lindy, wore a pompadour, and experimented with make-up, Mom's girls adhered to tradition. Her mixture of the mortar of home, school and respect held us all together, as we each faced our responsibilities.

> **Clarie**: After Grandpa Jacob died in 1942, Grandma continued to live with Julie, Jack and her children Marilyn and Ray in the first floor apartment. Those were the war years—in the world and in the house. When Julie gave birth to Robert Sheldon Cohen, the first male grandchild in the family who was also the first to have a middle name, it was virtually impossible to live with her.

Julie would dress up each day, apply a layer of make-up and strut up and down the street, pushing a high coach-style baby carriage. Bobby, a gorgeous, sweet-natured little boy with a mass of black ringlets, nestled against a pile of monogrammed, embroidered pillows and lavish quilts.

Julie rarely got along with Marilyn, and envied Grandma's close relationship with her daughter. Marilyn who was indeed "Grandma's girl," was also adored by Mom, and she lovingly called her "*tantequita* (auntie)."

As she matured into a bright, attractive, slim, college educated student, Marilyn found that her mother was competing with her. Consistent nagging even turned her husband Jack, a basically good guy who liked his mother-in-law, into an enemy. When Marilyn died of cancer at the young age of 45, her *tantequita* grieved for the child she had helped to raise, and thought of as one of her own.

In the midst of these family wars, Jack would periodically lose his job at the Waldorf Astoria where he worked as a room service waiter. He landed the well-paying job as the result of a strike, when he was hired as a scab and worked under the name of Jean Lemoine, a name considered more elegant than Jack Cohen.

Fluent in French, with a desire to please and a strong work ethic, Jack found a place for his abilities in the hotel which catered to the international set. During lay-offs, it was his sister-in-law Marguerite, who would go to the hotel, begging and pleading for her brother-in-law in French, explaining his need to work and support a growing family.

"Julie was a disappointment for Mama who could have used some help in sharing many hardships," said Charlotte. Instead, her sister proved to be an additional burden, causing Grandma and Mama great grief.

> **Clarie**: Eventually, after many altercations between the "upstairs" and the "downstairs," tempers flared, bitter words flew back and forth and Grandma moved upstairs to live with her daughter in relative peace, where she remained until she died. It never dawned on anyone to have her live anywhere else.
> My father, a difficult man treated his mother-in-law with great respect, knowing that she would not withstand

his volatile temper. Fully aware that his wife led a hard life, he also understood that among her few pleasures was the closeness of her mother, who helped with cooking, sewing and, more importantly, companionship.

During the war years the house was full. Mama cared and cooked for everyone, did the laundry and cleaned. Faced with food shortages and rationing, with coupons needed for everything, including leather shoes, she not only stretched a budget but her imagination to "make do."

While Essie was away each day, Mom, who had raised four daughters and provided emotional support for Julie's three children, managed to take care of Jerry who was not only frail but, in the family tradition, a poor eater. Essie and I contributed to the household budget when we were both employed full-time.

In spite of the extra load of work, Mama never compelled us to do chores but insisted that we concentrate on school and read books. We would help out by setting the table or washing and drying dishes, always singing the latest popular songs in unison. Together, any routine chore translated into an opportunity for laughter.

Sonia, Marie's oldest daughter, used to visit often, showing off a new dress, describing a boyfriend or venting her anger over the behavior of one of her brothers. She didn't have a sister and relied on "the girls" for companionship. In the late 1980s, when her only son faced serious problems, and her mother had died, Sonia, with no where to turn would show up at the house on 64th Street with a box of pastries.

The smile on her face would quickly turn to tears as she bent down to kiss "Margarite," and in minutes the pain spilled out. "*Tienes que hablar mi amor o un gusano va crecer en el cuerpo,*" said Mama, "you have to speak, my darling, or a worm will grow within your body." To Mom tears and sorrow were not a measure of weakness but something we all shared. Like her mother, she was always ready to listen to personal tragedies, and help heal the wound, before it turned into a *gusano* that could destroy the soul.

"Essie and I visited her in the hospital as she was dying of cancer, said Clarie. "Like Rebecca Bendina, who was part of my mother's life, Sonia was one of the sisters of our heart."

Left to right: Valerie Kubie, Ethel Kubie, Michelle Nahum,
Marguerite Sananes, and Clarice Nahum in 1965.

More Memories

CLARIE REMEMBERS

Clarie was the family artist. *"Trava de su padre,"* Mom would say, when she lapsed into assigning good and bad attributes to what she believed were inherited characteristics, and Clarie's talent was magical for her. *"Cada una a su oficio,"* she would insist, each according to her ability.

> **Clarie**: When I graduated from Washington Irving High School as an art major, I decided to look for work immediately. I wanted to assist Mom financially and buy nicer things for myself. I remembered how difficult it was for Essie to land a job before the war. With men in service I had an opportunity to find decent employment. It was not only a good decision, but a good time to launch a profession.
>
> Nevertheless, it was Mom who encouraged me to continue studying and I enrolled in Pratt Institute, where I studied at night for three years. She loved everything I designed, and when I was between jobs, anxious and dejected, she gave me moral support.
>
> Later, with a demanding full-time position as art director at Saks 34th Street, and evenings spent at school, I didn't see too much of the family. Slogging home near midnight, without dinner, I knew a hot meal would be waiting for me.

Mom was obsessed with marriage and security, baggage from the old country that she couldn't shed in the light of a new life and new values in America. If Clarie broke up with a boyfriend, she would get very upset. For her even *nombre de casada*, just having been married, was better than *mosa vieja*, old maid. The specter of spinsterish Aunt Ida hovered over the lives of Marguerite's daughters, almost like a fate worse than death.

Clarie: I met Gino Nahum, an accountant from Tripoli, at the Sephardi Club in Manhattan and we married in 1950. Our first apartment was a studio in the Sheepshead Bay area. Except for holidays and occasional visits, our busy schedules didn't allow for too much contact with the family.

In 1954, when Michelle was born, we moved back to Bensonhurst. From that day forward we all drew closer. Julie finally moved out of the ground floor apartment on 66th Street and Essie, Morris, Jerry and three-year-old Valerie moved in.

Each afternoon I would visit with my baby. When I went back to work for a short time in 1956, it was my mother who took care of Michelle and grew to love her.

After Joyce was born in 1959, I found it difficult to pick up Michelle for lunch each day and Mom would not only prepare a hot meal for her, but walk her back to school. To this day I appreciate what she did for me and my children.

The bond grew even greater when Essie took on a full time job with Citibank. Every morning, rain or shine, she would either come to my house or I would stop in to see her. We would do our marketing, stroll on 18th Avenue, greet neighbors and stop in one home or the other for a cup of coffee and a long, quiet chat, before proceeding with the demands of the day.

The moment we learned that Joyce had been accepted to a medical school, I rushed to the phone and informed my mother; I knew what it would mean to her.

Through the years, we shared our ups and downs, although I felt she suffered in silence too often.

170

A misdiagnosed severe case of poison ivy almost killed her and was later followed by a hospitalization for severe pain. To this day the cause remains a mystery.

Gino and I started Arrowpack, our own cosmetic container business, in 1980. A void was left in Mom's life as Essie and I became absorbed in our jobs. I phoned each day and visited on weekends, but we were aware that she was alone too often.

As the generation gap began to grow wider, we began to disagree on many issues, but I carefully avoided anything that would make her unhappy. Her health declined rapidly after a major illness in 1989 and it was agonizing to watch her mind slip away, as she died painfully, slowly. I hope that in these periods of her silence, she knew that my heart reached out to her.

When Mama merely communicated in cries and moans I heard her calling, "Help me to end my suffering." All I could do was sit at her bedside, stroke her thinning hair and speak softly to her.

This wonderful woman guided me through troubled times, giving me courage when I needed it. Through Mom's pain, the sisters have come together once again. Although we married, raised families and went our own way, we saw each other more regularly on her behalf during this crisis; we still have one thing in common, we loved her.

I ALSO REMEMBER MAMA

Her name fit her to a tee. She wasn't Meg, Madge, Margo, or Margie but Marguerite, a distinguished French name with a hint of elegance.

Never in her wildest dreams did Mom imagine that her children would be educated or attend graduate schools. One would earn a Ph.D., a grandchild would teach at Harvard and doctors, lawyers, artists, bankers, teachers and writers would populate the family.

My personal revolution against starting school and leaving the comfort of home became part of Mom's storytelling anthology.

> **Mom**: Gloria was my baby. It was hard for her to get used to school. The trouble began in kindergarten when Mrs. Grumberg ignored her and sat her in the back of the room with slower children.
>
> The teacher was a fool who never realized that she could read. By the time she went to first grade it became a big problem with vomiting each morning.
>
> At first we would bring her home, then decided that she had to get used to school. Marilyn who took her by the hand each morning carried a big towel to wipe up the mess.
>
> *Cuando echaba la fiel cada manana* (threw up or literally spilled her guts), Marilyn would clean up and leave her at the classroom door, with a very cooperative teacher who realized that she was a bright child. It took several months until she was willing to go without giving us any trouble, and she was never frightened again.

For a child who was school phobic I became a school addict, taking classes and earning degrees into my mid-50s, teaching at various schools for 30 years. The handling of the phobia was not only an example of wisdom and family healing, but a lesson in patience, *manana le pasara*, tomorrow she'll get over it. Mom had good sense, didn't panic, and instinctively knew that some children were afraid, needed time and didn't have to be labeled for life. I'm sure consultations with her mother, recalling who was afraid of school back in Salonica, and lessons from the past played a part in what to do with "the problem."

"No comes en la calle, no vale nada," she warned. Food in restaurants could kill you! Before federal controls, it could. But, I was always a wanderer and in 1947, at the age of 13, I bought a hot dog at a local deli and ate it in secret delight.

I thought mother was right as I retched for hours. Dr. Nathan Wilensky came in the afternoon. "Food poisoning, she'll be alright," he said as he sat down for a few minutes in his hectic schedule, and caught up on the local gossip with Mom who was one of his earliest and favorite patients.

But I wasn't any better, the pain in my groin got worse and the vomiting was relentless. Wilensky made a midnight call to the house where I lay on the living room couch as Mom paced the floor.

"Mrs. Sananes, it looks like appendicitis; it's not the hot dog's fault," he said, as he headed for the phone.

Mom woke up Daddy, "Joe, we need money right away to pay the doctor for the operation." We had no health insurance. The idea of waiting for bills wasn't considered.

Dad counted out $300; she stuffed them into her handbag as we both got into the doctor's car for the midnight run to Israel Zion Hospital. The next day I was up and about, and the family came to visit with a gift—Monopoly.

I was overwhelmed. That gift was and continues to be precious to me, one of the most tangible expressions of their love since they didn't believe in buying toys and dolls, that was for *bovos*—dopes!

Charlotte invited her college friends to play a few games with her baby sister and the healing took place. One week later I was back in my eighth grade class at Shallow Junior High, and Carl Messinger, the assistant principal, announced to the class that I was a brave girl coming back to school so soon. I had no choice—school came first in our house, if you could stand up and walk, you went to school..

Dr. Wilensky was also a friend. Mom knew him as a poor boy who struggled to become a doctor. She always fed his ego by recalling the old days when he waited in vain for a patient to enter his small office. He charged us $1 a visit and Mom, who never made an appointment, would just run across the street whenever she needed help. He understood us, who we were and didn't pass judgment.

The doctor had a good relationship with Charlotte who began to work as his assistant in 1943 and stayed on all through college. He admired her intelligence and followed her career.

My cousin Marilyn and I also worked in his office during our college years, but he never liked us very much, and paid us no more than fifty cents an hour for tiring work.

Marilyn was sloppy, couldn't afford to professionally launder her uniforms daily on a tiny salary, and on several occasions talked back to his wife who was a snob. Ruth Wilensky was condescending to Sephardim and had little use for us except as low paid helpers and occasional babysitters. Dr. Wilensky, accompanied by his wife, attended Charlotte's wedding in 1948 and mine in 1954. He enjoyed these poor people affairs, had a chance to see his patients, and found it relaxing. It also reminded him of his boyhood on 66th Street when he fought the medical school quotas against Jews and struggled through the trials of becoming a physician. Although he later prospered at a posh Flatbush office, he held on to the dark, dingy satellite on 66th Street, a reminder of the hungry years and the people who gave him his first break.

It was a sad day when Nathan Wilensky died in his early 40s as a result of complications from high blood pressure. Mom missed him terribly, *"un mansevo, un dotor,"* a young doctor who was part of our family. He was overworked, sick and constantly striving to earn more money, a sure recipe for a short life.

Every job we ever took was thought of as worthy, from testing urine for the young doctor, to a professorship in a prestigious university. Earning one's living was dignified. To this day I would rather mop floors on my hands and knees than beg for anything, from anyone. I never asked for help from my parents; it was demeaning, and though I valued the few things they gave, I saw it as an obligation.

In 1946, the year before I had my appendix removed, Mom was hospitalized for a partial hysterectomy followed by radiation therapy. It wasn't routine in those days and I was terrified of losing her. I helped at home and visited her each afternoon. She didn't gush over me, praise me to the skies or exaggerate what I did; it was expected and held its own intrinsic reward.

I was entering junior high. By summer's end, when she recuperated, Mom took me shopping for new school clothes and this time asked me what I wanted; without looking at the price tag, I picked a reversible raincoat. Unfortunately, the temperature hit 85 on that first day of school, and the coat rested on its hanger till October.

As an added bonus, she took me to the local hairdresser for my first perm; a big step towards independence, as I was allowed to leave the baby braids behind and join the family, having proved myself a responsible pre-teen. The tight curls might have looked like the result of electric shock, but it was a change and any break in routine was a high for me.

It was on a late August day in 1949, the summer I was 15, that I borrowed a friend's English racing bike. Within the first five minutes cycling down a sidestreet, I lost control hitting the non-existent footbrake instead of squeezing the handbrakes, and careened into a small truck.

Taken in a state of shock to Dr. Scovner, he looked over his rimless glasses and said, "It's a broken collar bone and a few broken ribs." The only solution was to immobilize the area and tape the ribs.

Mom felt a cold chill whenever she was obligated to call George Scovner, a "medical man" from the top of his homburg to his highly polished shoes. He was no Nathan Wilensky; we were merely patients to him and he looked down on the Sephardim and some of their old world habits. "What's the matter with you people?" he once said, after taking my temperature. "Don't you even have a thermometer?" Mom's cool lips against our brow seemed to register the slightest fever with amazing accuracy!

As much as I was in pain and shock, I was more concerned about going back to New Utrecht High School for the fall semester.

The driver, Mario De Bella, a short, stocky Italian man, was devastated; he had no auto insurance. He and his wife came to a meeting with my parents, old country style. Both families got dressed to impress the other and sat down at the dining room table for a cup of coffee and the required *rosquitas*. After the mandatory chit chat with exaggerated hand gestures, the discussion finally led to the responsibility for the doctor's fee. The couple agreed to pay the $40 bill and the two families parted as friends who would often greet each other when they met in the market. Imagine the years of litigation, bitterness and lying it would cause today with lawyers jockeying for position, a settlement and a large piece of the insurance pie.

I returned to high school that fall emaciated and a physical wreck. I took a crowded city bus each day and the only accommodation for my injury was an extra set of books to keep at home until my arm healed. I never missed an assignment or played the victim; it wasn't expected. At home I was allowed to complain, and I did have one long, drawn out crying jag, but in true Sananes fashion, I got over it.

Mom loved the dating habits of American girls. When I got calls for dates, she was delighted. Imagine finding husbands without matchmakers. Nevertheless, who the boys were and the family they came from was very important.

I met my first real boyfriend, Myron, when I was 15. At 6' 3", blond, blue-eyed and full of fun, the 17-year-old "Yiddish" caller from Coney Island was a breath of fresh air in our house. He walked down the street with a confident strut, laughed easily and told jokes. According to Mom, "*No es hathroso y tiene el aire del Americano,*" he wasn't a braggart and had the aura of an American. When describing him to Rebecca, she would say, "*que mansevo. Nos hizo patladeyar de la riza* (what a young man, we were busting our sides laughing with his jokes)."

The bubble burst when I causally mentioned that Myron, an early victim of a broken home, quit high school and was looking for a job to help support his mother. I thought I had dropped a bomb, as she looked at me in horror. The prince instantly turned into a frog. "What, a school dropout? You aren't going out with him anymore; it's finished and we won't even mention it to your father."

It was with tears in my eyes that I watched Mom meet Myron at the front door on the following Saturday night, when she told him directly, "You are a nice fellow, but I will never let my daughter go out with a boy who drops out of school. When you get your diploma, come back."

He telephoned many times after that, although he never got his diploma. My tears dried, my anger died down, Mother prevailed and in retrospect she spared me a lot of heartache.

Over the next few years dozens of boyfriends walked up the staircase to a reception in the dining room, where they were eyed carefully. Among them was Bernie, who's mother was chronically ill; Larry a wannabe actor; Josh the handsome airline pilot; Norman an engineering student; Jack a spoiled rich boy; Roy an Englishman; Vic the sailor; and Ruby, who was too shy to reach out and hold my hand. But Mom never had to take charge again. They all had their high school diplomas and most were nice Jewish boys.

When I applied to college, Mom knew I wasn't as gifted as Charlotte but felt that in a year or two I could meet an acceptable future husband. As time progressed and I did well, she insisted that I graduate. "You're making Bs," she said. "I won't let you drop out."

I recall trying to impress her with my wisdom, as I read aloud a term paper in psychology filled with the pseudo-knowledge of the freshman. "*No entiendo* (I don't understand it)," she said in awe. Then I realized a growing arrogant attitude, and another lesson was learned, simpler is better.

When I told Mom that I wanted to marry Arnie Stein, she said, "He's a nice boy, good natured and intelligent, but poor. I want to ask your father." Dad, having earned money, lost money and suffered the consequences, answered in father-knows-best American fashion, "I like him, he comes from a good family, he's smart and good natured. She should marry who she wants; money is not the main thing." That was it! The necessary approval was given. It was a decision Mom was never to regret for one moment, and neither did I.

I can't recall Mom taking a nap or relaxing. Up before we woke each morning, she went to sleep only after we were all safely in bed. She rarely sat down to eat, preferring to serve. My father would get furious. "Marguerite, would you sit down goddamit!" he would shout when food was dished out and everyone had dived in.

There was no full-length mirror in our house. Mom, who had no time for primping, was never given to fads, facials, fashions or mood swings. More than her fear of aging or death, which was inevitable, was her dread of becoming a burden to her daughters or facing a long life without security. Sometimes I felt that she was obsessed with security, making ends meet when it was no longer necessary.

Home provided a sense of place and a sense of purpose. It only bothered her when something had to be fixed and either Dad wouldn't do it or refused to hire a professional. Then, although she encouraged us to own a home, she would lament, *"casa es dolor de cabeza* (a home is a head-ache)."

In her 90s, when Mom broke her hip for the third time she looked up at me from her bed at the Hospital for Joint Diseases in Manhattan and said, "Gloria, when I leave this place and go home, I'll never leave my house again." I agreed with her, it was enough!

Occasionally, Mom would sigh, "What would I have been if I had been raised here." Then she would look at us contentedly and know that her dreams were realized in our goals, lives, expectations.

Hers was a world of books and ideas, as she celebrated those like herself who triumphed over hardship. She thrived on rags to riches stories, especially chronicles of self-made millionaires that didn't forget where they came from.

THE NEW HOUSE AND MANY GRANDCHILDREN

After Grandma died in 1964, the two-story home on 66th Street became a burden for Mom who found it more difficult to deal with winter snow removal. "The house was badly in need of repair and we decided it was time to look for another home to share together," says Essie.

The decision to leave the home where she had raised her children wasn't easy, but it was time to go. The smaller row house only two blocks away on 64th Street had a separate second floor apartment which was to be occupied by Mom and Jerry, while Essie, Morris and Valerie set up housekeeping in the main living quarters on the ground level.

It took Mom almost two years to adjust to her new smaller home, and she would often sigh about leaving her *casa spaciosa*, but as she became immersed in the life on the block she gradually felt more at ease.

"The neighbors on 64th Street were very friendly," said Clarie. Fanny Dolchek, a neighbor, was married to an evil man. She would periodically come to visit Mom, wringing hands and wiping tears as she would commiserate on the problems of marriage.

Over the years Fanny was joined by a continuous line of women friends, including Susie Cresco and Anne Del Valle. One of her favorites was Renee Altair, a spirited woman married to a Native American, who would lean back in a comfortable seat on the sunny front porch, sip a cup of hot coffee and tell the story of romance and marriage to an interesting man who preferred to strut around barefoot.

On morning walks through the community Mom would often stop and chat with neighbors who respected and loved her. It was in this home that she had more free time to enjoy and experience the closer friendships that were lost when she left Salonica.

> **Clarie**: While Mama was bedridden for years, people stopped me on the street to ask about one of the sweetest, most caring women they knew. Mama's ministrations didn't stop with older local women venting their souls; she helped young people in special situations.
>
> After Valerie married Dr. Bob Sable she was visited by Bob's sister Marilyn, a serious French student. During a study year abroad in France, Marilyn boarded with Madame Delabre in Paris, and became close to her hostess. It was Mom who later helped the young student correspond with her French friend and eventually Madame and Marguerite also exchanged letters.
>
> When Marilyn married and invited Madame to her wedding, Delabre traveled to Brooklyn to meet her pen pal, and the two embraced like long lost friends.

Mom loved to speak, read and write in French; it was the language that helped her step out of *el cortijo* and into the world. She would often begin one of her lessons in life with, *"el Frances dice,"* and, of course, it had to be true! One of her favorites was an old adage, on *Honi soit qui mal y pense* (evil is as evil thinks).

Sometimes when we were feeling badly over some incident, she would hasten to remind us that *apres le pluit, le bontemps* (after the rain, comes good weather), wisdom that emerged from the French Revolution.

During the 70s and 80s, as she became less active, Mom would spend many hours in the slatted sunlight of the porch, reading, crocheting, listening to the radio or watching the street scene when her eyes were tired. Occasionally she would tune into "Edge of Night," a late afternoon soap, but she always claimed *"que era una bava,"* a lot of nonsense, when compared with the real life stories she heard daily.

At her feet she kept a stack of library books and a cloth bag with crochet projects in progress, afghans for her daughters or grandchildren. We keep her labors of love as life-long treasures.

> **Clarie**: Mama was not a religious woman; her religion was manifested in the way she lived by the Ten Commandments. We instinctively honored our parents, never stole a thing and to my knowledge never coveted anyone else's husband. She always reminded us to think before we acted and not *trae verguenza a la familia* (not to shame the family.) I don't think that she ever hurt or cheated anyone in her entire life, and was always willing to accept the short straw.

There's a strong link between Clarie's feisty daughter Joyce and Mom (probably the reason she chose to specialize in geriatrics).

Clarie: On the day Joyce was born, as she was caring for Michelle, Mama met up with a neighbor, Anne Shapiro, and the conversation turned to a recent dream in which Anne met her daughter Frances who had died at a young age of multiple sclerosis. Learning that I had just given birth to a little girl, she asked if there was even a remote chance that I would give my infant her daughter's name.

Gino and I had planned to call our baby girl Joyce Marguerite, but Mom, who didn't take dream messages lightly, relinquished her name to bring joy into the life of a grieving mother, and our daughter was renamed Joyce Frances.

On Joyce's birthdays, Mama would take her to visit Anne Shapiro who lived in a nearby apartment house. Arriving with a kosher cake, the trio would have a private celebration. Anne died when Joyce was four years old, but we occasionally call her Frances, and remember the mother, her daughter and the difference a little kindness can make.

Joyce recalls Halloween costumes sewn on the hand-operated Singer sewing machine Mom used for over 70 years. It is now stored in the basement. She sewed for school plays and helped Michelle with unique design projects.

MICHELLE

"Grandma has been with me all of my life; I grew up with her, my aunts, and my cousins," says Michelle. "We fulfilled her dreams: college educated, independent, professional women, prepared to earn our own way in life. The house on 66th Street was a big house to my small eyes, with two stories and six gray steps leading up to twin front doors reserved for company; but we used the alley entrance.

Living was easy all summer as we played on the stoop with a pink rubber Spaulding ball, sat on the bench and talked to neighbors, or watched the boys play street stickball.

Mr. Todero, the immediate neighbor, was familiarly known as "Papu." He didn't like kids playing in the connected alleyway and, with an old fedora perched on his head, strode up and down the area protecting his turf. We were warned to avoid problems with him.

During the late 50s and early 60s the junkman still came down the street with a horse and wagon, and the ice cream truck brought kids streaming out of their homes when it rang its bell on the twice daily visits.

Grandma took care of her mother who we referred to as "Menachi," a form of *manna*. We loved and respected Menachi because our Grandma and our parents did. The older woman occupied a small room at the back of the house near the master bedroom. Although crippled and bedridden she was an important part of everyone's life until she died at the age of 95. She even predicted her death to the day and my Mom, Clarie, often remarks that she speaks to her in dreams.

Valerie, Essie's daughter, and I weren't allowed to attend Manache's funeral because we were too young. The house seemed so dark that day, maybe it was because the two of us were alone, separated from the family.

Grandma was always making an afghan or mending

something while she told stories of our history in Spain and life in Greece. There were a couple of old mouton fur coats from the 40s in the closet and since it was the 60s we thought wearing them would be real cool.

Valerie especially begged to wear one of the coats to school. The old furs were split from age, wear and tear, but Grandma found a big needle and sewed her fingers sore, making them wearable until they tore once again.

About Valerie: Mama loved taking care of new born babies, observing the budding of life before care and caution creep in. Valerie was one of the joy's of Mom's life. Sweet, good natured, beautiful and kind, she came at the age of three to live in the family home on 66th Street when Essie and Morris moved out of a housing project, and was often described as *los ojos de Ester* (Essie's eyes, a very strong expression of love meaning that this child was as important as one's sight). Her admission to the High School of Performing Arts (the school acclaimed in the movie *FAME*) partially fulfilled Essie's theatrical dreams, and especially Mom's, who saw a star on the horizon.

Valerie didn't make it to Broadway but finished college and became a teacher of the deaf. Everyone was just as proud of her.

Although Mom never came to parents' meetings at P.S. 205 when we were growing up, she became more involved with the school life of her grandchildren and even attended PTA meetings at the prestigious high school. "The dance instructor was impressed by her beautiful legs," Essie said. "You should have been a dancer, Mrs. Sananes." Mom loved that!

Valerie was one of the few people Essie and Morris agreed on. They came together to attend her school functions or to accompany her to special events. At 18, she married Bob Sable, a graduate engineer from MIT and a medical student. It was a fantasy realized for both Mom and Essie; Valerie had done it. Without a bank roll and a big trousseau, she had married well.

Jesse, Valerie's first child, was born when the couple were both busy with careers and lived on Pelham Parkway in the Bronx. Recently Jesse followed in his father's footsteps and graduated with honors from MIT. He is currently employed by Bloomberg News Service.

The failure of Valerie's marriage may have been the reason for Mom's unexplained illness and hospitalization in the late 1970s. In an ironic twist Dr. Bob Sable was her attending physician. As she looked at Valerie's husband, her pain penetrated even deeper. But, she got over it and Valerie went on to marry Kenny Koppelman, a young teacher she met at John F. Kennedy High School in the Bronx who is now a successful lawyer.

Valerie, Ken, Jesse and their son Andrew now live in a majestic mini-estate in Tarrytown, New York.

JAMES, JOSH, JON, BOB, AND CAROL

Charlotte married Joe Russell, a successful attorney, in 1948. After living in student housing on North Brother's Island (former isolation hospital area) in the Bronx, the couple lived in a housing project until they finally moved to a succession of better apartments in Manhattan. Mom did not have as much of an opportunity to visit with Charlotte's children Jimmy and Josh as she did with the Brooklyn grandchildren.

Nevertheless, in spite of advancing age she would trek to Washington Heights to visit her children and grandchildren. The long subway ride from Brooklyn to Manhattan took over an hour and a half and she would tote bags full of good things to eat for lunch.

After I was married and moved to the Heights near Charlotte's apartment, we would all get together for lunch when Mom visited, and shared the bountiful goodies which often included, *fijuelas, ensalada de cebollas, fijones, y pimentones fritos*. Those get togethers, as we dipped crusty semolina bread in the onion salad, beans or fried peppers were a delight, as time disappeared and we were all together back home.

Josh was born when Jimmy was four years old. Six weeks earlier I had given birth to Jonathan, and Charlotte and I shared babysitting. As she was recuperating from a Caesarean section, with a new-born infant to care for, Charlotte and Joe learned that four year old Jimmy had an obstruction in his kidneys and required surgery.

Mom trudged back and forth on the subways to help care for Joshua, as she and I tried to help Charlotte through this nightmare.

Jimmy, a professor at Harvard University, and a scholar in eastern languages loves his Grandma and some of the delicious things she made for him.

> **Jimmy**: Grandma told me that she had been a labor organizer in Salonica and that the newspaper which e employed her was also published in Hebrew script. I remember when she babysat with me and made "Greek Chow Mein;" anything with lemon juice was Greek!

She gave me Grandpa Joseph's psalm book which was given to him by the Rabbi of Tetuan, Morocco when he emigrated to America.

In 1993, while I was teaching for a year in Israel before coming to Harvard I returned for a short visit to the US and went to see her. She didn't recognize me. Essie explained that I was Jimmy, her grandson, a professor in *Yurushalayim*. "Ah," she said, and spoke to me politely in French.

The following week she told Essie that she met a pleasant gentleman, a professor from Palestine. I sensed that her mind was in the Ottoman Empire where Israel was Palestine and the only people you called professors were doctors. Back in Jerusalem, I passed the old gates of the Alliance school and recalled my wonderful grandmother's early years that were hopeful and sometimes quiet, before all the dispersal, war and holocaust.

Although I visited the family in Brooklyn periodically, Mom only came to know my children, Jon, Bob and Carol, on her visits to Manhattan. Shortly after Grandma died she would occasionally join us on a day trip to a public garden or the seashore. For many years after a trip to Hershey, Pennsylvania, she recalled the town's street lights, in the shape of chocolate kisses.

When I was sick with a serious infection following Carol's birth, Mom once more trudged to visit me often via the subway. When the children were ill and I couldn't take more time off from my teaching job, she would stay with them, tell them stories and bake goodies. Jon recently found a recipe for *fijuelas*, and makes them for his family.

As much as we loved and praised our children, she would go further in showing them off, insisting *que la abuela es doz veces madre* (a grandmother is twice a mother!).

"They are so smart and beautiful," she would say, *el grande* (Jon) *se asemeja* (looks like) a Errol Flynn, *y Bobby es el para el dio como mi padre* (and Bob was an answer from God

188

like her father, Papa). Mom saw Carol as a beautiful, wonderful gift to me. She would often say, *"Me allegro que tuvites una hija."* Mom finally appreciated the importance of having a daughter.

TO EACH HIS OWN

To Mom and Dad we were never lumped together as "the girls"; each one had a distinct identity. We barely resembled each other, and had diverse interests and goals. Charlotte bears the closest resemblance to Mom in appearance and character. I often wished I looked like her, so that I could retain a small piece of my mother's love in my reflection.

Mom never wanted us to travel. *Mejor en casa, algo te pasara, que es la ajile?* (Home is best, something may happen to you. What is the hurry?) "Why go anywhere else, when New York has it all." I had a crazy wanderlust that bordered on the bizarre. If a plane flew overhead I wanted to be on it, if someone described a trip, I wanted to walk in their footsteps.

Clarie and Esther weren't obsessed with seeing the world and took trips conveniently at leisure. For Charlotte it all came a little more naturally with professional success.

"Tienes un culo de mal asiento (You are restless)," Mom would sigh as she watched me spend hard earned dollars on mere pleasure. While I have settled down somewhat at the ripe age of 62, I still read travel accounts with the relish others get from watching their investments soar. I visualize myself and Arnie trekking through jungles, rafting down rivers or talking to people who might speak in click tongues.

Mom worried that if we traveled we could be in danger, and she was afraid to lose us. As I watched her diminish, I felt

189

that she never lost us; we were always there for her. Essie remained close to Mom most of her life, and for the past 40 years they have lived together.

> **Essie:** I had a hysterectomy in 1986 when my mother was 86 years old.
>
> I had divorced Morris in the late 1970s and Mom, Jerry and I now lived as one household. For six weeks she tirelessly nursed me back to health.
>
> Our relationship was such that no matter where we were, we were together in spirit. Intelligent and educated she was aware of world events and she remained my constant companion and best friend all of my life.

In her 90s, Mom had a third fall that broke her femur and escalated a retreat into a dome of twilight. Essie, Claire and Charlotte took her to a dozen specialists for care and consultation, to relieve the constant pain. After a year the doctor offered two options; amputation or a lifelong cast. "To me amputation was not an option," said Essie, "and I felt that if he could create a flexible two-part cast, I could keep her leg clean, we would consider it."

Ultimately, Mom didn't walk and Essie removed the cast. The leg never withered, although during the last two years of her life before she passed away in 1997, she lost contact with people and place. Through it all Essie worked relentlessly to hold together whatever life she could before she and Mom were pried apart.

> **Essie:** To see my mother, who was my confessor and my strength, decline had a strong effect on me. God gave me willpower that I never knew I had, as I marshalled my abilities, physically and mentally to manage 24-hour care with many lost hours of rest.

Nevertheless, I saw to it that she had a nutritious, tasty diet, was comfortable and clean in a caring, loving environment.

Over the years my sisters tended to go their separate ways, but with Mom's deteriorating illness, we became close once again; sharing our past and our present.

Left to right: Grandma (Rachel Benruhe Saltiel), Marguerite, and Essie, in 1953.

A Few Final Words Before A Sad Farewell

What did our mother teach us? We learned that a wonderful life has pleasure and pain, with many highs and lows. We discovered that you lose some battles and win others, and losing meant *"capara,"* just forget and move on. She insisted *que no hay mal que por bien no sea*, which translates to the popular concept that often failure presents new windows of opportunity.

The sound track of my mother's life included door bells announcing visitors, sweet songs in Romance languages, rhythm, clapping, lullabies, soft words of kindness, and sighs of love lost and found, as she consistently wrapped us in her blanket of warmth.

In a disordered war-torn life she sought order. From dislocation, she sought roots. Imprints of her past in the tradition of Jews as people of memory left space for us to draw courage, as we marched at the head of our own parade.

Traditional insecurities and struggles faced by women, Jews and immigrants in particular, led her to abandon self-fulfillment for a piece of the American pie. What began as a young woman's desire to write for the public was turned around as the result of war and the destruction of a home.

Rather than pine for what might have been, Marguerite's early dreams switched to an immigrant's reality: marriage, children and devotion to *las hijas* (her daughters).

To us she was a hand to hold in the night, a cook, washerwoman, an ironer of clothes that had to look right "this minute." Much of her prime was spent making ends meet in days marked by savings and sacrifice, yet she was within reach for each of us at any hour of every day. From lives of scarcity we have all attained a life of abundance and realize that "things" can never replace the satisfaction of understanding ourselves and others.

Before penicillin became the panacea, Mom was the bearer of mustard plasters, the lips that kissed feverish brows, the arms that cradled our babies as she cradled us. She was our adviser, defender, mother of our motherhood, the shoulder which sopped up our tears and the arbiter of our rage when we sought someone to blame. She was our inspiration and at times our desperation.

We often took her for granted, didn't always listen when she spoke, smugly stating that her old world was too far away, just a collection of reminiscences. Yet, as daughters, mothers and wives with different experiences, we often traveled and tripped on the same roads. Ladino expressions continue to spice our language, thoughts and dreams. It punctuates moments of frustration, pleasure, love, humor and anger.

In the final years, her circle of life and proud posture led to a limbo of misery, as she inhabited a world devoid of day or night. Seeing our mother fade is like watching the sun; you never think it will disappear. She was the buffer who separated us from our fear of aging, and she no longer exists.

193

Left to right: Mom, Essie (in back), Clarie, Joyce (Clarie's daughter) and Charlotte (in the front).

In America, the elderly aren't revered as a wealth of folklore and wisdom but blamed for social security depletion, a burden on the health care system and a problem for their children who become the parent of their parent. Mom told us that our roots indicated royal blood, as heirs *de reyes y reinas* in medieval Spain, but for us, she was the real queen, and her legacy has remained strong. Like the small pebble thrown into water, creating ever increasing ripples, her life has found a safe space in the hearts of our family.

Mom asked Essie to read this poem
by Alfred de Musset at her funeral:

Mes cheres amis
Quand je mourais
Plantez une saulaie
Au cemetaire
J'ammais son foliage
Et Pleurais
Sa paleur et douce
Et chere
Et son ombre serais
Leger a la tombe je dormerais

My dear friends,
When I die,
Plant a weeping willow
In the cemetery.
I love her foliage
And mournfulness.
Her pallor is sweet
And dear.
Under her airy shade
In a tomb, I will sleep.

BIBLIOGRAPHY

Angel, Mark. *The Jews of Rhodes: The History of a Sephardic Community.* New York, Sepher-Hermon Press, 1978.

Editors of American Heritage. *The American Heritage History of World War I.* New York, American Heritage Publishing Co., Inc., 1964.

Ausubel, Nathan. *Pictorial History of the Jewish People.* New York, Crown Publishers Inc., 1953.

Benardete, Mair Jose. *Hispanic Culture and Character of the Sephardic Jews.* Second ed. New York, Sepher-Hermon Press, Inc., 1982.

Hamblin, B. Colin. *Ellis Island.* Santa Barbara, Calif., 1991.

Marks, Copeland. *Sephardic Cooking: 600 Recipes Created in Exotic Sephardic Kitchens from Morocco to India.* New York, Donald I. Fine, Inc., 1992.

Megas, Yannis. *Souvenir: Images of the Jewish Community: Salonika, 1897-1917.* Athens, Kapon Editions, 1993.

Rodrigue, Aron. *Images of Sephardi and Eastern Jewries in Transition: The Teachers of the Alliance Israelite Universelle 186-1939.* Seattle, University of Washington Press (undated).

Rodrigue, Aron. "The Sephardim in the Ottoman Empire." *Spain and the Jews; The Sephardi Experience 1492 and After.* Ed. Elie Kedourie. New York, Thames and Hudson, 1992, pp. 162-188.

Sciaky, Leon. *Farewell to Salonica: Portrait of an Era.* New York, French and Europenan Publications, Inc., 1946.

Sevilya, Metin B., M.D. "The Psychological Aspects of Sephardic Identity." *The Sephardic Scholar Series 3* (1977-78): 75-82.

America 1920-1930.

America 1930-1940.

America 1940-1950. Time-Life Books, 1969.

Weich-Shahak, Susana. *The Judeo-Spanish Vocal Reperatory-Context and Functionality in Sephardic Society.* 7/4/95. E-mail address: webmasters@music.ed.ac.uk (Hebrew University of Jerusalem).

NEWSPAPERS AND NEWSLETTERS AND JOURNAL ARTICLES

Angel, Mark. "After the Expulsion: Aspects of the Sephardic Spirit." *Congress Monthly*, 59 (1992: p. 10-15).

Bedford, Bob. "The Fire in Salonika." *Sephardic Home News.* Brooklyn, New York, 1992.

Bohlen, Celestine. "Silence Ends and Jewish Ghosts are Remembered." *The New York Times* Apr. 1997 International ed.: A4.

Bowman, Steven. "Notes on the Jewish Military Reputation in Greece, 1914-1935." *Jewish Museum of Greece Newsletter*. Athens, 1989.

Bowman, Steven. "Jewish Medicine in the Balkans Before 1500." *Jewish Museum of Greece Newsletter*. Athens, 1992.

Halio, Hank. "Ladino Reverie." *Sephardic Home News*. Brooklyn, New York, Sept. 1992.

Hassid, Sam. "The 1920 Elections and Salonika's Jews." *Jewish Museum of Greece Newsletter*. Athens, 1994.

Meyer, Sari. "A Study Tracing Salonican Surnames to Spain." *Jewish Museum of Greece Newletter No. 31 & 32*. Athens, 1991, 1992.

Levenson, Gabriel. "Two Milennia of Judaica Survive in Modern Greece." *Jewish News*. 28 Dec. 1989: 28.

Riding, Alan. "500 Years After Expulsion, Spain Reaches Out to Jews." *The New York Times*. 1 Apr. 1992, late ed.: A14.

Shepard, Richard F. "Sephardic Jews Mark 500th Anniversary." *The New York Times*. 30 Mar. 1990: C17.

Philologos. *On Language. Jewish Daily Forward*. 12/96.

Young, James E., "Lands of His Fathers." Rev. of *The Cross and The Pear Tree: A Sephardic Journey by* Victor Perera. *New York Times Book Review*. 9 Apr. 1995, p.16.

Spain—Ministerio de Informacion y Turismo *1971 Espana Gastronomia: Espana, Un Lujo Alcance.*

CORRESPONDENCE

Makris, Lambos. *Thessaloniki*. E-mail address: LMAK@eng.auth.gr

The author's children in 1987 (left to right): Jonathan, Carol, and Robert Stein.

197

THE AUTHOR

Gloria Sananes Stein, an award winning educator and freelance writer, is the co-author of *Tips From Top Teachers* and *Country Legacy: Lancaster County One Room Schools*.

She has written fiction and nonfiction, has been published extensively as a newspaper and magazine correspondent in Lancaster County and in other areas of Pennsylvania, and has taught writing on the college level.

Gloria is the mother of Jonathan, Bob, and Carol and resides with her husband, Arnold, in Holtwood, Lancaster County, Pennsylvania.